The Anti-Liberal Manifesto

The Anti-Liberal Manifesto

Letters to the Left from a Conservative Commoner

H. J. Willoughby

LIBERTY HILL PUBLISHING

Liberty Hill Publishing
2301 Lucien Way #415
Maitland, FL 32751
407.339.4217
www.libertyhillpublishing.com

Paperback ISBN-13: 978-1-6628-3140-9
Ebook ISBN-13: 978-1-6628-3141-6

This book is dedicated to my husband, my children, and
to freedom-fighting patriots everywhere.
God bless you.

Table of Contents

Preface

THIS BOOK IS being written by a commoner. I do not have any claim to fame, nor do I have any such ambition. I am a wife, a mother, a blue-collar worker, and a student working on my fourth degree. I was raised poor and have worked my ass off to become middle-class. Over the last twenty years, I have witnessed a shift in the cultural and political dynamics of our great nation, and it is very unsettling. We have gone from American pride to a country filled with raging lunatic freedom haters. We went from sweeping unity on 9/11 to sympathizing with the dickhead terrorists that killed almost three thousand innocent Americans

And while the travesty of what we are becoming fully enrages the patriots that still remain, it has become over-whelmingly evident that this cultural metamorphosis is not occurring by chance. There is no paradigm shift in the American way because people have become "woke" to some bizarre new reality. This wokeness and attempt to overturn the United States of America has been carefully planned and laid out by the global cabal who have invested deep into the pockets of the Democrat party. They are exploiting unknowing Americans as pawns through mental manipulation and impassioned hysteria. They understand that dividing the people makes them weak, and they are targeting us right where it counts—race, gender, family, religion, and the freedom of our American culture. They are using everyday citizens to accomplish the destruction of our personal liberties. These everyday American's have been convinced that our country was founded on racism, hate, and White supremacy. But what these American's don't realize is that this woke revolution was crafted by billionaire globalist liars who are hell-bent on manipulating Americans with their emotions to put an end to their freedoms. This anti-American revolution must be stopped.

President Donald J. Trump had a comprehensive understanding of this attempted coup. He knew the job wasn't going to be easy, but he stepped up to the plate and began the nasty job of "draining the swamp." The political offices in Washington are held by countless traitors to the US, working tirelessly to overturn our government. President Trump recognized this and knew he needed to throw a wrench in their plan. The ridicule, the lies, the mockery, and the repeated attempts at impeachment didn't faze him, and making America great again meant removing these treasonous assholes from office. And while some of us had a solid appreciation for what Trump was boldly doing, the mindless masses stared at their television's night after night, and their empty heads were filled with leftist Nazi propaganda. They bought the fake news.

They believed President Trump was a racist, misogynist, and a xenophobe as a result of the masterful deception by the liberal media giants. Lie after lie after lie was told about

Trump, and the pre-scripted opinions of the globalist puppet masters were belched into living rooms across the US every single day. The pro-America message President Trump delivered hundreds of times made the corrupt Democrat elites' skin crawl. They realized that he was starting to undo what they had begun. Millions of Americans started to wake up and feel a deep love and loyalty to their country. Patriotism was on the rise, and people from every race and culture were uniting in the name of freedom, justice, and liberty once again!

Well, that just wasn't going to do. The globalist Democrat party and the liberal Nazi funders invested millions and millions of dollars into hate groups aimed at dredging up discord, angst, and destruction. Race became the focus and theories of "White privilege" cast a shadow over our freedom, pointing blame at White-skinned folks for just existing. Their goal is simple: destroy America at any cost.

When Biden stole the election, the globalists scored big. They had placed a warm body with dementia into the highest office in our country. He was the perfect stooge, a simpleton tool who would do or say anything they wanted (if he could spit it out), and in exchange, they would cover for the evil of his past, as well as the filthy and treasonous acts of his cracking-smoking whore son, Hunter. Biden's undeniable racist past, his violation of women, his pedophilia, his corrupt business dealings with foreign countries, and the contents of his slimy son's laptops would all suddenly cease to exist. The globalist's mission is clear, and with the help of Biden, an unstoppable sequence of economic disasters has been launched.

Their economic agenda includes:

- Break the economy by printing trillions of American dollars, resulting in the catastrophic plummet of its worth. Inflation, inflation, inflation.

- Raise taxes on everyone.

- Force American businesses President Trump brought back to the US by to move out of our country, where production is now more affordable.

- Make US energy dependent on the Middle East when we were energy independent for the first time ever under President Trump.

- Break the people.

- Break the unity.

- Break this country once and for all.

And just as the "conspiracy theory" of Covid-19 starting in the Wu-Han lab was proven true, the stolen election "conspiracy theory" will soon validate President Trump to be 100 percent right, once again. The liberal left, who lack any trace of morality, are not above stealing an election from the American people. It doesn't matter what BBC, CNN, MSNBC, CBS, *The New York Times*, or any other Nazi-left publications say. They've all been bought. They do not report news. They peddle propaganda. They are the liberal Nazi media. They all lie, manipulate, and gaslight. They are complicit in this treason.

And while the bogus mainstream media dummies fawn over Biden, making revolting excuse after excuse for the racist gaffs and daily incomprehensible mumblings, they fail to report on the undoing of our freedom. They have been paid to focus on the drudged-up racism of White Americans and law enforcement, and over-report on the "Capital Riots" as a means of dividing our country even further. They have been well compensated to disseminate stories that destroy what lies at the very heart of America—unity.

This book is meant to give a voice to all the commoners in our country who recognize what is going on and who want it to stop. We are told that the way we can make a difference is with our vote, but when that is greedily stolen from us, we are left with nothing but red-blooded rage. I, for one, will not sit idly by and watch my great country get swallowed up. I wrote this book to confront the callous liberal henchmen, carrying out the sinful wills of the global elites as well as the everyday liberal sheep that unknowingly support the dismantling of the last true front for freedom in our world. While there may be some points in this book that a few free thinkers may disagree with, I believe for the most part that this manifesto sums up the collective thoughts of most of us.

I hereby pre-call out you jackasses before you attempt to say this book is racist—*you are racist*. This book clearly proves that anyone that contradicts anything that I say in the book is deeply and fundamentally racist at the core of their very soul. This book is not propaganda. I do not belong to "Q". I am not a right-wing extremist. I am not a conspiracy theorist. This book is not "dangerous," as I can clearly hear countless brainwashed libs say. I have not been bought like the media puppets or anyone else. I have not swallowed the propaganda. I represent the majority of people in the United States of America, and I stand for liberty, for racial equality, for freedom of speech, freedom of thought, and for every single one of our Constitutional rights. I boldly stand against socialism, communism, globalism, and wokeness. But most of all, I stand with Jesus Christ who died for the sin of every single man and woman on earth, regardless of how vile and pitiful they are. He alone brings true unity.

Unity is freedom.

CHAPTER 1

Dear Liberals,
You are all Karens.
Sincerely,
Logic

SORRY, INNOCENT PEOPLE named Karen out there. That was a sucker-punch some of you don't deserve. But there is currently no more accurate way to describe the narcissistic mind-set of the liberal left who are loud, pushy, virtue-signaling hypocrites. As we all know, the term "Karen" was originally intended to describe a pushy White woman who is racist, entitled, and uses her privilege to demand her own way. This might come as a shock, but most liberals are racist, entitled, and use their liberal privilege to demand their own way.

We've spent the last several years listening to leftist extremists push radical views on the public that are in staunch opposition of what is ethical, what is good, what is kind, and what is. These zealots have distorted history, indoctrinated youth, violated morals, slandered the innocent, and have convinced some that communism is better than freedom. Naive Americans are falling for the liberal plan, packaged as virtuous and marketed as truth. With this deception, the Karen elites are calling the shots. They've complained. They've bullied. They've called management. And they are manipulating the American people with their liberal privilege to get their own way.

These Karens have managed to cultivate a climate in which anyone that opposes their radical liberal views gets called a "radical." Anyone who dares call out the hypocrisy gets called a "hypocrite," a "racist," a "bigot," an "extremist," or a "danger to democracy." And don't you dare offer another point of view or you will be called a "conspiracy theorist." It is nothing short of gaslighting on steroids. On January 6, 2021, Americans were told that the Capital siege was motivated by Trump supporters, yet the fully staged spectacle suggests heavy Democrat planning, entirely contrary to the media's anecdote. Liberal politicians wasted no time creating yet another false narrative, depicting those who supported Trump as "dangerous," "radical," and "fascist," and the masses gobbled up the fiction. Months later, with full intention of furthering the leftist fantasy, feebleminded Joe Biden called the events of that day the "worst attack on our democracy since the Civil War," entirely negating the horror of September 11, 2001, and countless other nightmares that are burned into the memories of red-blooded Americans.

Karens, like Joe Biden, Nancy Pelosi, Bill and Hillary Clinton, Barack and Michelle Obama, liberal loud-mouth celebrities, liberal media activists, Jack Dorsey, Mark Zuckerberg, and Bill Gates (to name a few), have used their power and entitlement to gain more control and to exploit the American people. Their end goal is to change our country into a globalist hole where American's freedoms are entirely gone.

This vomitous "wokeness" has infiltrated all aspects of our lives. We can't even watch professional sports anymore without a clump of multi-millionaire elitist brats taking a knee because they feel so "oppressed." This wokeness makes most Americans gag and is exactly why the ratings have plummeted so drastically. In fact, NBA Finals were down 50 percent in viewership compared to the year before ([1]). Americans just can't seem to dig down deep enough to sympathize with these privileged elites. They just want to watch a basketball game without "wokeness" overshadowing the sport. And we get it from every direction—sports, news, music, movies, TV shows, and so on. It is a constant barrage of woke preaching, and it sucks ass! Americans are starting to enjoy hearing that the Oscars, the Academy Awards, and the Golden Globes ratings have all plummeted. We know it's bad when American's are cheering that the woke American Olympians lost to another country. That is music to our ears for so many of us who are disgusted by these privileged aristocrats. We don't care about your rich, pompous-ass, totally out-of-touch opinions. We can't stand you! We don't want to hear you tell us what to think, feel, or believe. You can suck it for all we care!

So why, exactly, is this "wokeness" so out of control? The investments made by George Soros have profited him well. This Nazi Jew is a billionaire world elitist that has set out to destroy America and anyone who stands in his way. George Lombardi writes that "George Soros is anti-God, anti-family, anti-American, and anti-good. He killed and robbed his own Jewish people. What we have in Soros is a multi-billionaire atheist with skewed moral values and a sociopath's lack of conscience. He considers himself to be an elitist world-class philosopher, despises the American way, and just loves to do social engineering, and change cultures." He went on to say Soros has been actively working to destroy America from the inside out for some years now.

People have been warning us. Two years ago, news sources reported, "Soros is an extremist who wants open borders, a one-world foreign policy, legalized drugs, euthanasia, and on and on. This is off-the-chart dangerous." Does any of this sound familiar? Open borders? Legalized drugs? In 1997, Rachel Ehrenfeld wrote, "Soros uses his philanthropy to change, or more accurately deconstruct the moral values and attitudes of the Western world, and particularly of the American people." His "open society" is not about freedom; it is about license. His vision rejects the notion of ordered liberty, in favor of a *progressive* ideology of rights and entitlements." (²) In 2008, Soros donated 5 billion dollars to the Democratic National Committee to ensure Obama's win. By doing so, he could undo America from within. Matthew Vadum wrote, "The liberal billionaire-turned-philanthropist has been buying up media properties for years in order to drive home his message to the American public that they are too materialistic, too wasteful, too selfish, and too stupid to decide for themselves how to run their own lives." (2) Richard Poe writes, "Soros' private philanthropy, totaling nearly $5 billion, continues undermining America's traditional Western values. His giving has provided funding of abortion rights, atheism, drug legalization, sex education, euthanasia, feminism, gun control, globalization, mass immigration, gay marriage, and other radical experiments in social engineering." (2) If you wonder why these messages have been crammed down our throats for the past ten years, look no further. George Soros has purchased control of the Democrat party and they have become his anti-American pawns. Half of America is buying into the ideology of a literal Nazi. The same half that calls pro-America Trump supporters "Nazis." Can you see the irony here? The hypocrisy is staggering.

To achieve this globalist objective more quickly, leftist news hacks have been employed to carry out the daily dirty work. The liberal media has become a full-blown propaganda machine. Prefabricated opinions are peddled by wretched puppets who should be called "actors" rather than "journalists." Trump repeatedly called them "fake news," and time after time he was proven right. Yet the phony stories that the media must walk back are always kept on the down-low and usually get small print on the back page. The thespian "news" parrots dictate what Americans should care about, believe in, who they should hate, who they should love, what they should support, and, of course, who they should vote for. The brilliant *Project Veritas* exposed the lies of CNN with their own director admitting on camera to advancing propaganda, but of course the mainstream outlets won't be showing these clips ([3]). Talk shows and late night "comedians" get a host of fake laughs with their incredibly not-funny jabs at anyone and anything that is in opposition to the left. And *The View* should have been pulled years ago. Those skanks are some of the most ignorant personalities on TV. Most of America is dumbfounded by the stupidity these moron's spew. I can only assume from their ignorance that they get direct deposit from Soros himself. Seriously out of touch and ignorant. Embarrassing.

One of the most frightening realities of the media's repugnant reporting is the actual identical resemblance to Nazi media in the 1930s and 1940s. Liberal Democrats insist that President Trump and his supporters are "Nazis" for having American pride, while the left uses Hitler's playbook to brainwash the masses. Mainstream "news" and entertainment have all aligned to generate the same identical stories (propaganda). Censorship is at an all-time high. Opinions, books, stories, brands, and people are censored, doxed, threatened, harassed, and slandered by the liberal Nazi Karens of today's America. The events that are actually occurring in the U S and around the world are altered and overshadowed by exaggerated tales that run on a loop. It is said that repetition is a powerful tool that convinces people to believe what is being recapitulated.

The media simultaneously regurgitates hundreds of liberal fabrications, such as "police are inherently racist," echoed by celebrities, athletes, and even the most ignorant president of all times, Joe Biden. *Facebook, Instagram, Twitter,* and other social media sites have become "social activist" sites, censoring anything that goes against the left's propaganda. The public buys the narrative, and just like that, millions of mindless drones become extremists for the "cause" the left tells them they should have. When President Trump was in office, the flavor of the day was the mistreatment at the border of illegal immigrants, but with a Democrat in the charge, the same treatment of these migrants (and worse) is ignored. The media pushed the "Me Too" movement, only convenient if it supports a Democrat accusation. Don't forget climate change, followed by Covid, all intertwined with racism. If you hear it from mainstream media, you'll soon hear an army of passionate sheep declaring the injustices of "today's special." And they didn't come up with the tiniest bit of it on their own.

Karen wants her way. Karen demands it.

The missile exchange between Israel and Palestine in May of 2021 set the stage for liberal Nazis to rear their ugly heads once again. For those of us who actually learned true facts about World War II in our history classes, the Nazis under the lead of Adolf Hitler set out to murder as many Jews as they possibly could. Hitler once said, "For us, this is not a problem you can turn a blind eye to—one to be solved by small concessions. For us, it is a problem of whether our nation can ever recover its health, whether the Jewish spirit can ever really be eradicated. Don't be misled into thinking you can fight a disease without killing the carrier, without destroying the bacillus. Don't think you can fight racial tuberculosis without taking care to rid the nation of the carrier of that racial tuberculosis. This Jewish contamination will not subside, this poisoning of the nation will not end, until the carrier himself, the Jew, has been banished from our midst." ([4]) That's some pretty sick stuff.

So on May 11, 2021, when Palestine launched rockets at Israel, liberals everywhere rallied in favor of Palestine after Israel defended itself from these vicious attacks. Anti-Semitism around the world skyrocketed once again as liberal activists screamed in defense of Palestine. Kuhner writes, "Most progressive Democrats are not only anti-Israel, but deeply anti-Semitic. As Hamas and Islamic Jihad rain rockets and missiles on civilian areas across Israel, the Democratic Left has openly done something once thought unthinkable: embrace Palestinian terrorism" ([5]). The very group that flagrantly accuses Trump and his supporters of being Nazis are blatantly condemning and attacking anyone of Jewish decent. The anti-American, anti-Israel bimbo Congress woman Ilhan Omar tweeted, "Israeli air strikes killing civilians in Gaza is an act of terrorism. Palestinians deserve protection. Unlike Israel, missile defense programs, such as Iron Dome, don't exist to protect Palestinian civilians. It's unconscionable to not condemn these attacks on the week of Eid." (⁶) This lying sac of crap, Omar, failed to mention Palestine initiated this war. Her anti-Semitic rhetoric helped to motivate hate crimes against Jews around the world.

"In Washington DC, Black Lives Matter protesters marched while chanting 'Israel we know you, you murder children too' and at an anti-racism rally in Paris inspired by Black Lives Matter, protesters wore T-shirts reading 'Justice for Palestine' and waved Palestinian flags while chanting 'dirty Jews' as they marched. This is happening and is a common occurrence at Black Lives Matter protests across the country and around the world." (⁷) And who is funding these BLM protests? None other than the anti-Israel Jewish Nazi himself, George Soros.

To distort reality and evade the truth, the liberal media is doing it's very best to try to pin the anti-Semitism on Trump supporters. One CBS article stated, "A number of pro-Trump rioters who stormed the Capitol wore clothing with anti-Semitic messages—the latest sign of a growing problem in America" (⁸). What this incredibly ignorant journalist isn't comprehending is that Trump and most of his supporters are about as "pro-Israel" as you can get, and the incomparable support Trump gave Israel during his presidency is proof. Clearly that CBS professional liar didn't realize they were outing the Antifa and BLM plants in the crowd that day. Trump and his supporters understand that Israel is our ally. We do not support terrorism of any kind, and we condemn nations that support terrorists. For many of us who call our-selves Christians...we will always have Israel's back.

In 2018, President Trump withdrew US funding for Palestinians and began a peace process that focused on normalizing relations between Arab states and Israel. The program was so effective that Trump was nominated for the Nobel Peace Prize. Flights began between Israel and the UAE for the first time, and the UAE offered congrat-ulations for Israeli Independence Day. Bahrain and even Saudi Arabia were brought into more normal relations.([9]) But anti-Americans like Ilhan Omar commanded Biden to undo the Middle East victories made by his predecessor. One month before Palestine attacked Israel, in a complete reversal of President Trump's accomplishment, the Biden administration announced $235 million in aid to be sent to Palestine. Um, did Biden just fund Palestine's attack on Israel? The timing is awfully suspicious! Who wants peace? Not the anti-Semite Nazi left. It will never be enough for Palestine until Israel is gone.

Recently *Breitbart* published an article magnifying a perfect example of liberal anti-Semitism. "Kamau Bobb, *Google's* global head of 'diversity strategy and research,' and senior director of the 'Equity in Computing' research center at Georgia Tech, claimed that Jews have an 'insatiable appe-tite for war and killing' in a 2007 blog post on his per-sonal website." ([10]). But his sentiment from 2007 is nothing new and is ramping up around the world. "Reps. Ilhan Omar (D-Minn.), Rashida Tlaib (D-Mich.), Alexandria Ocasio-Cortez (D-N.Y.), Ayanna Pressley (D-Mass.), and the newest member of "The Squad," Cori Bush (D-Miss.), all took to the floor of

Congress last week to falsely accuse Israel of "war crimes" and being an "apartheid state." Their diatribes there and elsewhere, including on social media, have helped create an atmosphere where hatred for Israel has become not merely fashionable, but obligatory for many on the left" ([11]).

Ilhan Omar has refused to condemn Al-Qaeda, the militant Sunni Islamist multi-national terrorist organization that is responsible for the 9/11 attacks and downplayed these attacks in a speech at Ground Zero as "some people did something" ([12]). Rashida Tlaib comes under frequent fire for her anti-Israel sentiment. She is an avid supporter of CAIR, an organization created by and publicly in support of designated terrorist organization Hamas ([13]). Hamas is the second largest terrorist group in the Middle East and is responsible for the May 2021 attacks on Israel. Yet the "squad" blames Israel for defending itself. Their hate has contributed to the rising anti-Semitism world-wide through misleading, false anti-Israel rhetoric. And, of course, the biggest bimbo of them all, Alexandria Ocasio-Cortez, had to chime in on something she clearly knows nothing about, calling Israel an "apartheid state" ([14]). She obviously does not know that it was Palestine that rejected statehood three times ([15]). Americans agree, AOC, you contributed more to society as a bartender. Go away!

In the 1960's and '70's, the liberals embraced the "hippy" movement. The movement promoted peace, non-conformity, was anti-war, and anti-establishment. Yes, a lot of it was annoying as drug use was celebrated, as well as rebellion against the middle class, but some good came of it too (well, actually just the music). This movement turned into a lifestyle for many, and these hippies slowly morphed into what they hated—the pretentious middle-class, sometimes even upper-class who assume that they know what's best for all Americans. These boneheads who fought against the establishment have become the establishment, worshiping corporate America, voting in war-monger presidents like Obama and Biden, and virtue-signaling at every turn.

These mouth-breather liberals have officially become the antithesis of what hippies in the 1960's stood for. They postulate that they know what the United States needs to bring peace and justice while turning a blind eye to the absolute destruction these Antifa and BLM assholes are bringing to small businesses throughout the U S. They have embraced hate and only "love" the ideologies they promote. "Make love not war" has mutated into "make war until you meet our demands." This mass hysteria is not condemned by liberal Democrat politicians. No way. It is promoted and even fueled to cause further conflict and breakdown of the American way. And their venom against anything that they don't agree with has clouded their ability to see that they are annihilating America for future generations. Globalism means zero freedom, zero rights, and no hope—exactly what the global cabal wants.

America has been called the cultural melting pot of the world. As a people, we have had struggles from the start, but as a nation we have worked together to unite as a collective force. The Civil Rights movement of in the 1960's put into motion enormous strides in the fight against racism, and great progress was made in racial equality. But the Democrat party, coerced by the global cabal, are actively working to undo all the progress made by great leaders, such as Martin Luther King Jr. The drummed-up cries of racism rake in dollars for the DNC, funneled through groups like BLM, and the families of Breonna Taylor wonder where the support is for Black lives now. The Democrats perpetually deceive the masses and shamelessly use minorities as instruments for political gain. Identity politics is the corrupt avenue they use to rake in more votes. Radicalized Democrat leaders pander to the masses, telling them they are victims of capitalism and of the Constitution, and ignorant citizens buy into this scam, accepting the promises of a better life, only to be screwed over after election day. The cycle never ends.

The past several years have brought about a very alarming phenomenon. Liberals (ironically, the name implies freedom) have whole-heartedly embraced mental captivity. They love to condemn anyone who thinks differently. They are not above slander, defamation, destruction of property, alienation from society, and extermination of anyone with a view that opposes their own. Varying perspectives used to be taught to encourage critical thought, but today's privileged liberals get to dictate what is moral, just, and ethical with nothing but disconnected premise and emotion-based appeal. The First Amendment, intended to safeguard Americans from mental, verbal, and written oppression, has come under full-blown assault from the left. Through bullying and virtue-signaling, liberals have positioned themselves in a place where they decide what truth is, regardless of fact and reality.

If you voice disagreement, you are censored. This phenomenon is furthered by the douchey mainstream media who dish out the phony "truth" and create an entirely false narrative to Americans. This mental slavery begins when an individual starts to question their own thinking, based upon the outline the left has given them. It is gaslighting at its finest. "If I don't say I have White privilege, I am a White supremacist." "If I believe that all lives matter, I am a racist." "I need to use the right pronoun for that person, or I'll be doxed."

Citizens of the greatest country that has ever existed have been convinced that they are fascists if they have any American pride. They are convinced they are racist or privileged just for being born White and told they are dangerous radicals for wanting to uphold the Constitution. Americans have opened the door to mental captivity, have closed the door behind them, and have dropped the key into the sewage drain in the middle of the mental prison cell. They are afraid to think differently for fear of being stormed by the liberal mob. Fear of losing business or government funding fuels this captivity in both large- and small-scale arenas. And the irrational, emotional-based ideologies that have been infused into American culture have begun to infiltrate every facet of our lives.

Corporate America, healthcare, the military, law enforcement, small businesses, public schools, churches, and even some private schools have all been threatened into obedience. Policies in each of the aforementioned entities have been changed to appease the left. If they don't satisfy the mob, financing will be lost, credibility with be shattered, and their organizations will be lambasted as "haters." Those on the left who hold positions of leadership in these organizations parade themselves as the blameless elect and rewrite protocols that endanger the livelihood of anyone who disagrees. Mandatory vaccinations is a perfect example. Anyone who verbalizes anything that is paradoxical to the liberal global agenda or the hate-filled scheme to destroy America is at risk. Anyone who represents true American freedom and all that the American armed forces fought for in the past is almost guaranteed to be censured. The First Amendment has never, in the history of our great nation, been in such great jeopardy as it is now. Taking the remarks of conservatives out of context has become an art, yet those same remarks and worse, if said by a liberal, are praised and called heroic. The liberal Democrat's hypocrisy has evolved into a relentless, unholy monster.

Another example? There are many, but one of the biggest and most hypocritical illustrations that has enraged every tenacious, truth-seeking American is the blatant smear campaign the Democrats, the mainstream media, and liberal celebrities barraged us with the Capitol riots. It does not take a rocket scientist to understand that the malicious and corrupt Democrats wanted to frame Trump in hopes or impeaching the man. They were not the least bit hesitant to spend millions of our tax dollars on attempting to impeach a president who was no longer in office. They ramped up the hate all over the news, and the American sheeple became enraged at anyone who backed Trump. They labeled it an "insurrection" and convinced millions of knuckleheads that there was a planned government coup that day, which once again, was proved to be untrue. Yet the events of that day emboldened liberals with a blood-thirsty animosity for anyone that disagrees with them, and the fake news continued to fuel the anger with ludicrous, bogus narratives. Heinous politicians like Maxine Waters *literally* scream at crowds that they should "get more confrontational" at BLM protests, but because she's a cold, barbarous Democrat, her disgusting hate-filled dictates were overlooked. Yet Trump was and is still being crucified for his words that were given meaning unintended on that day. It's nothing less than mob mentality.

The left has lost their collective mind. This blatant attempt to frame Trump and his supporters as terrorists is one of the most colossal scams of the left to date, yet the multi-million dollars of damage to cities across the U S, which was induced by none other than the anti-American Antifa and BLM groups goes unchecked. Those are "mostly peaceful protests" according to the media liars. Then we have dumbass AOC who is said to be getting therapy because of the PTSD the Capitol riots caused her, when she wasn't even in the building where the riots took place! Seriously embarrassing. And the "January 6 Commission" which is the brainchild of that vile Pelosi wench, is just further example of the desperation that the Democrat leaders must continuously discredit and slander any and every conservative. Why? Because we stand in the way of globalism.

Trump and American patriots screwed up their globalist plan. If you try to do your own research, you'll find a slew of leftist media outlets, condemning anyone who doesn't support the January 6 Commission. The liberal fascist search engine, *Google*, censors out most other reports. Let's not mention that the same corrupt politicians that pushed the whole "Russian collusion" lie are the same corrupt politicians who wanted the formation of the January 6 Commission. Shouldn't we find that to be a bit suspicious? The enormity of the Russian collusion scam cost millions and millions of American tax dollars and was nothing more than an expensive smear tactic on the American people's dime. But let's not investigate the corrupt ties that Joe Biden and his slutty, drug-snorting son Hunter have with Communist China, or the incredibly seedy involvement Hunter had with Ukraine while Daddy was vice president. Again, nothing to see here! The countless corrupt doings of leftist politicians that go unchecked are nauseating. Many Americans are waking up and are tired of the gaslighting. Americans are not stupid, like Hillary Clinton says we are. These liberal elites have been bought and are controlled by the globalists. They must annihilate anyone or anything they are instructed to destroy. And their propaganda has convinced the sheep of their plan.

This mob mentality that has possessed foolish youth and young adults to riot, burn down buildings, destroy historic property, and topple down statues that represent our country's past has infected the feckless liberal Congress. Our own Congress of the United States of America is littered with anarchists who cry "racism" if you disagree with their anti-American sentiment. Well guess what, Rashida Tliab, We the People take *great* offense when you verbally attack our police force with your filthy hatred. These men and women represent every race and have trained hard to serve and protect everyone, including idiots like yourself. Proclaiming that law enforcement is "inherently racist" shows your lack of intelligence and your anti-American passion. You are a treasonous witch, anyone that holds an elected office in the United States of America *must not* be anti-American! Any Democrat politicians and Republicans in name only (RINOS), who idly sit by with their mouths open and drool dripping down their ridiculous faces, *must* stop conforming to these insolent terrorists. There is no level of intimidation or dirty money that should stop them from wanting to save our country from the grip of anti-Americans like these radical, nightmare terrorists who have infiltrated our government! Fools like Cory Bush who honestly believe the American people should not have a police force to call upon for protection, yet who spend thousands and thousands of dollars on their own personal security should be elected out of their positions of power. Disgusting.

And this goes, too, for other senseless clowns holding state offices around the country. The mayor of Portland, Ted Wheeler, writes, "We believe in the power of government to work for all Portlanders. We work to build a community that enjoys economic prosperity, a healthy environment, affordable homes, and a safe place to live and thrive." ([16]) I choked on my coffee when I read that. *This guy is a joke*! He took office in 2016 and has literally watched his city unravel and transform into a third world hell hole because he is a liberal coward who bows to the globalist agenda. Elected officials like this pansy-ass are afraid to stand up to the anarchists running rampant in the streets.

President Trump offered to send federal enforcement to take down that embarrassing "autonomous zone," and

Wheeler said, "No thanks"! This arrogant asswipe would rather pander to liberal bullies and let Portland spiral into a filthy cesspool than to have accepted help from President Trump. Think about that. And then the liberal boobs who elected him (and reelected him) wonder why their beautiful city is falling apart, why their property values are plummeting, and business is moving out. Hmmmm, I wonder!!!

Then these same boobs who keep electing Democrat cretins into office can't figure out why their taxes are so high, why their schools suck ass, and why their cities are so dangerous. Why homelessness is skyrocketing in their cities, and hardcore drug use continues to soar. Why used needles and feces line the streets and tent cities are taking over what used to be tourist destinations. So, they move to Republican-run cities where the taxes are low, the schools are better, and crime isn't anywhere close to where they came from. And they continue to vote Democrat! We're watching Californians evacuate to Texas and Idaho, and New Yorkers fleeing to Florida, and these red states are at risk of flipping blue! This proves what Dr. Michael Savage said to be undeniably true: "Liberalism is a mental disorder." We are watching our country turn into a hole, just like George Soros wants.

Tucker Carlson from *Fox News* put out a list of 100 things the left claimed were "racist' in 2017 ([17]). Please look this up. He gives links to his references so you can see this stupidity for yourself. The list is so idiotic and annoying—and a stretch, to say the least. But hundreds, if not thousands of things have been added to that list since. Pretty much anything that is American or belongs to American culture or way of living is "racist." And this is precisely how these leftist Nazi globalists are doing away with our way of living. Condemn it. Bully into silence. Control.

You, liberal numbskulls, have gone way too far. The American majority (who voted for Donald J. Trump in the 2020 election) find your ideologies and politics repulsive. We will never bow to your wokeness. We will never bow to your globalist agenda. We will fight for our Constitutional rights through hell or high water. Suck it!

Disclaimer: This chapter was not aimed at all Democrats. Many of you are moderate and continue to vote Democrat because that's just what you and your family have always done. It is crucial for you to realize that your party has boarded the fast train to globalism and is using the pretense of socialism as a dirty disguise. It is time for you to recognize the racist past of your party. You must realize that our country is in distress, and your freedom is literally hanging in the balance. Your party is not what you think it is.

CHAPTER 2

Dear liberal science "experts,"
Your message is a hoax,
Sincerely,
Critical thinkers who refuse to buy the
propaganda you're pushing

THE IRRATIONAL DISPOSITION of the left has permeated literally everything. A woman can kill a baby inside her womb and proudly brag, "It's my body, my choice," but the same argument isn't permitted for refusal of an EXPERIMENTAL vaccine. The hypocrisy is stupefying! There is 99.999999% chance that a baby will die in an abortion, yet there is over a 99 percent chance that an individual under seventy years old will survive a Covid infection. Those over the age of seventy have a 94.6 percent chance of survival. ([18]) Those are pretty good odds! But the survival rate and the very low risk of death for the population is swept under the rug, and fear is proliferated by the left. We never hear a peep from the "scientists" about building our immune systems, or about effective Covid treatments, and we never hear a peep about natural immunity after a Covid infection. Those scientists and medical doctors are heavily censored. Facts that don't back up the radical globalist agenda are called "conspiracies." These moronic, holier-than-thou virtue-signalers will berate anyone who refuses to inoculate themselves with a test serum, and the hype around it all is sickening!

The mainstream media has labeled those who refuse the Covid vaccine as "anti-vaxxers" and ridicules them as conspiracy theorists. However, most individuals who choose not to get the Covid vaccine have done their homework. They aren't buying into the fear tactics of the radical left. The media has declared the Covid vaccine is a means of preventing contraction of the virus when it is actually only meant to reduce severity of symptoms. ([19]) The left is bullying free thinkers and marginalizing anyone who is hesitant to get injected with this mass experiment. And while those who beat the doors down to get their Covid vaccine brag about how "safe" they feel, they sadly have no idea what the future holds for their health and well-being. Half of America doesn't seem the least bit concerned about the potential long-term effects of this injection. They have taken what the fraudulent Fauci says at face value and have done zero homework on their own. They fell for the fear mongering. And now we have new "variants" coming out every other day which will require "more" injections, none of which have sufficient scientific proof or peer-reviewed research to back up the efficacy. I don't trust the phony-ass science they are pushing, and it really doesn't take a rocket scientist to find any of this over-the-top vaccine-push to be suspicious! Yet the liberal left calls those who use critical thinking skills, "anti-American". Since when is freedom of choice "anti-American"? I'll tell you when. When the push for globalist control became priority number one.

Doesn't it seem the least bit curious that we don't hear about natural immunity for those who have had Covid? "Months after recovering from mild cases of COVID-19, people still have immune cells in their body pumping out antibodies against the virus that causes COVID-19, according to a study from researchers at Washington University School of Medicine in St. Louis. Such cells could persist for a lifetime, churning out antibodies all the while." (20) But the liberal politicians and media insist that every person on the globe should be vaccinated, even against their will. Countless people around the world are having adverse effects from the vaccine, and thousands have died, yet the media remains completely silent on this terrifying reality. They continue to call vaccine reactions or death "rare", but as a healthcare provider myself, I can honestly say it is anything but! For many Americans, it is hard not to have "vaccine hesitancy" about being part of a grand scale experiment when you understand that you are at serious risk for death or disability. Hard pass, thank you. Not to mention the extreme censorship and discrediting of physicians who want to discuss Covid treatment with medications like Ivermectin and Hydroxychloroquine. Heaven forbid we talk about something that has been proven to work!

The "heroes" of the healthcare world (doctors, nurses, respiratory therapists, radiology techs, etc.) now have a choice to get inoculated or lose their job. Talk about getting stabbed in the back! They were good enough to be used through the beginning of this Covid disaster with supply shortages, low staffing, and endless hours. They all rolled their eyes when hospitals and clinics across the nation planted signs out front that proclaimed, "Heroes work here!". They knew it was a marketing ploy. And here they are, about to lose their livelihood because the "science" just doesn't check out. What a joke.

Tucker Carlson on *Fox News* reported that the propaganda liberal news has made repeated claims that "White men" and "Trump supporters" comprise the largest groups of those who refuse to get the jab, and even go as far as to say that Black American s have some of the highest numbers of Covid vaccinations. Yet the actual numbers say the exact opposite. According to *KFF.org*, as of May 2021 when this paragraph is being written, 61 percent of the total White U S population have been inoculated, whereas only 12 percent of Black American s took the vaccine ([21]). Black American s historically do not trust the government when it comes to healthcare. This problem stems back to the Tuskegee experiments that ran from 1932 to 1972 and exploited the health of many Black Americans, killing over one hundred innocent men ([22]). By reporting these fictitious vaccination numbers, the mainstream media can target the biggest threat to the globalists plan: White male Trump supporters. If they can paint White conservatives as the enemy, as they are with the Capitol riots, they can begin to write policies that initiate segregation once again, limiting the rights of a select population. These tyrants are gunning to segregate our country again by race, by vaccination status, and by political views. This is precisely what the vaccine passports aim to do. What the Civil Rights movement did is being undone in a matter of months. The anti-freedom policies the left is pushing will be endless. It is racism and it is communism. Not exactly sure how the Democrats can deny how incredibly racist the vaccine passport is with the largest population of unvaccinated American's being black! It's maddening.

Recently, Defense Secretary Lloyd Austin said that the "most urgent challenge we face in the U.S. military is the pandemic." ([23]) What a joke! In 2020 there were twenty-six military deaths related to Covid ([24]). In 2020, there were 571 military suicides ([25]) ([26]). Can you really be that out of touch, Lloyd? You don't even know these stats? How disgusting. Yet politicians, officials, media, and propagandists push the same narrative. They want everyone vaccinated, and they're using fear like this as their motivator.

President Trump confidently proclaimed that Covid-19 was a man-made virus that was developed in the Wuhan laboratory in China. The media, the politicians, and celebrities went wild, attacking his claim as a conspiracy theory and mocking him (as usual) for making such a preposterous statement (and again, without proof of their own to debunk his remark). Yet one year later, we discovered that President Trump was, in fact, 100 percent correct in his assertion. In May 2021, Rand Paul, U S Senator from Kentucky, confronted Dr. Fauci on his hand in the "gain of function" research in the Wuhan lab. This research aims at producing "juiced up" animal viruses to infect humans. Dr. Fauci denied it, but his ties to the funding of scientists working on super-virus studies are glaring. ([27]) Funny, but scientists in India discovered four patents owned and invented by Dr. Fauci for man-made glycoproteins insertions found in the Sars-Cov virus. "We found 4 insertions in the spike glycoprotein (S) which are unique to the 2019-nCoV and are not present in other coronaviruses. Importantly, amino acid residues in all 4 inserts have identity or similarity to those in the HIV-1 gp120 or HIV-Gag, all of which have identity/similarity to amino acid residues in key structural proteins of HIV-1 is unlikely to be fortuitous in nature." ([28]). But this doesn't fit the narrative the globalists need to be pushed, so Americans don't hear this information. These Indian scientists were quickly forced to withdraw their studies, as this would clearly suggest that the Covid-19 virus was a man-made bioweapon with ties back to the director of the U S Institute of Virology and Infectious disease. Nothing to see here! And we are supposed to trust Fauci when he says the Covid vaccine is "safe and effective"? Funny how when Fauci's emails were leaked, the "conspiracy theories" of conservatives were proven true once again. Fauci is a criminal, and the radical left is complicit in these crimes against humanity.

And what about the anti-virus king Bill Gates coming out as a leading medical authority on the importance of vaccinations? This man, who is *not* a doctor, has been applauded for his vaccination expertise, yet anyone else who discusses the topic (i.e., Joe Rogan) ([29]) gets scourged for having an opinion without a medical degree. Americans aren't supposed to question this? Free thinkers are wondering why we should trust the "science" that changes every day. Free thinkers would like to know why they should take a vaccine that has had no long-term testing results. Free thinkers wonder why this vaccine is being pushed so hard when it didn't protect the population against the Delta variant and there is zero data on other variants popping up worldwide. Free thinkers are hesitant to get jabbed when the adverse reactions and deaths are being grossly underreported. And anytime anyone voices an opinion other than the vomit being spewed by mainstream media, it is called "propaganda." *The irony*! This is about control. This is about limiting freedom and punishing those who refuse to comply. This is about globalism. Hey sheep! Please keep getting your Fauci tattoos. Your proclamation of moral, ethical, and physical superiority is incredibly entertaining—pure comic relief!

When we look at the other fraudulent scientific hoaxes the left is pushing, one of the biggest of them all is "climate change," "global warming," or whatever else they call it to suit their agenda for the day. This charade, of course fervently fueled by the media puppets and pushed by the liberal elite, has been a looming theory, pushed as fact for decades. Yet none of the "predictions" made by these numb-skull idiot "experts" have come true. Not one. This list is abbreviated ([30]):

1967: "Dire famine by 1975" (*Salt Lake Tribune*)
1969: "Everyone will disappear in a cloud of blue steam by 1989" (*New York Times*)
1970: "America subject to water rationing by 1974 and food rationing by 1980" (*Boston Globe*)
1971: "New Ice Age Coming" (*Washington Post*)
1974: "New Ice Age Coming Fast" (*The Guardian*)
1974: "New Ice Age Coming Fast" (*Time Magazine*)
1974: Ozone Depletion a "Great Peril to Life" (*Time Magazine*)
1978: "No End in Sight" to 30-Year Cooling Trend (*New York Times*)
1988: Maldives completely under water in 30 years (*The Canberra Times*)
1989: Rising seas to "obliterate" nations by 2000 (*Associated Press*)
1989: New York City's West Side Highway underwater by 2019 (*Salon*)
2000: "Children won't know what snow is." (*The Independent*)
2002: Famine in 10 years (*The Guardian*)
2004: Britain to have Siberian climate by 2020 (*The Guardian*)

2008: Arctic will be ice-free by 2018 (*Associated Press*)
2008: Al Gore warns of ice-free Arctic by 2013
(*Wattsupwiththat.com*)
2009: Prince Charles says only 8 years to save the planet
(*The Independent*)
2009: UK prime minister says 50 days to "save the planet
from catastrophe" (*The Independent*)
2009: Arctic ice-free by 2014 (*USA Today*)
2013: Arctic ice-free by 2015 (*The Guardian*)
2013: Arctic ice-free by 2016 (*The Guardian*)
2014: Only 500 days before "climate chaos"
(*Washington Examiner*)

This is a shortlist of the ridiculous "scientific" predictions relayed through fake news publications to scare the world, and not even one of them was right. Idiots everywhere are counted as "experts" such as the obnoxious Swedish child brat now an adult brat, Greta Thunberg, who commands the world to comply with her demands. David Harsanyl writes, "Sixteen-year-old Swedish climate change activist Greta Thunberg lives in the healthiest, wealthiest, safest, and most peaceful era humans have ever known. She is one of the luckiest people ever to have lived. In a just world, Thunberg would be at the United Nations thanking capitalist countries for bequeathing her this remarkable inheritance. Instead, she, like millions of other indoctrinated kids her age, act as if they live in a uniquely broken world on the precipice of disaster. This is a tragedy" ([31]). Yet this response from Ms. Thunberg is precisely what the globalists what. To indoctrinate the world with fear, especially our youth. That way it will be all hands-on deck when they create impractical policies and laws that do away with our everyday freedoms.

In April of 2021, *Project Veritas* uncovered one network's phony global warming narrative when it secretly recorded CNN's Technical Director Charlie Chester discussing CNN's "Climate Crisis" town hall as a bad joke: "'Our next thing is going to be for climate change awareness ... That's our next pandemic-like story that we'll beat to death ... Fear sells." ([32]) And just as the fake news beat the world with the overblown Covid statistics, the global warming con is being ramped up again. How are American s being so easily swindled? These science authorities were telling us that the next ice age was upon us, and in less than ten years, our ice caps were slated to be completely melted away! A true climatologist, Judith Currey, writes, "If you don't support the UN consensus on human-caused global warming, if you express the slightest skepticism, you are a 'climate-change denier,' a stooge of Donald Trump, a quasi-fascist who must be banned from the scientific community." ([33]). So basically, any scientist that voices any opposition, in any way at all, is immediately discredited and shunned. Liberal Democrats are the anti-science party. No wonder the UN hated President Trump so much. According to a 2017 article on *Heritage.org*, the energy regulations agreed to in Paris by the Obama administration would destroy hundreds of thousands of jobs, harm American manufacturing, and destroy $2.5 trillion in gross domestic product by the year 2035 ([34]). As a businessman with a pro-America agenda, President Trump knew he had to pull the U S out of that ridiculous agreement. But, on

January 20, 2021, dumbass Biden rejoined the Paris Accord. America last. Globalist agenda first.

So, while actual scientists who understand that gas emissions are not responsible for the fluctuation in the temperature of the earth's atmosphere, countless voices in the science community are silenced because their message doesn't fit the narrative. And billions of American tax-payer dollars continue to pour into the cause, directed by the liberal elite. Science? Oh sure. There are plenty of scientists that lack a moral compass and sling whatever crap they are paid to sling—and the sheep of the world eat it up. Anything contrary is a "conspiracy theory." This is not to say that the temperature of the earth doesn't fluctuate. It has fluctuated regularly since the dawn of time. Real science has proven that time and again. So no, Arnold Schwarzenegger, the world does not need to stop eating so much beef as a means of preventing the "harmful damage" that farming does to the environment. Greenhouse gases have proven to have little to zero effect on the climate ([35]). And we aren't going to start eating insects as an alternative to steak! ([36])

The irony is that Democrats actually believe they are the "party of science." What a laugh! The party that endorses biological males competing against biological females in sports because of how they "feel." The party that thinks a five-year-old has the maturity and awareness to decide what gender they are but still need help tying their shoes. The party that endorses body-altering hormone therapy for adolescents, most of whom suffer from mental illness. Even the language, "gender assigned at birth" is a joke. That child's biological gender was determined the very second the winning sperm entered the ovum. There is no decision-making in this process. Gender is preordained by God. This entire liberal movement manufactures confusion about identity. And with that confusion, the leftists push identity politics used to manufacture votes to keep their anti-America agenda strong, involving no science at all, actually, just confusion, deception, and lies.

Women are taking testosterone and bulking up, growing beards, and dropping their voices a few octaves, but when they have a problem with their intact vagina, healthcare providers are forced to do a full-blown pelvic exam on a "dude." Men are taking body-altering hormones, chopping off their penises, growing boobs, and shaving down their Adam's apple because they feel like a princess. This body-altering mania is not addressing the issue at its heart. In 2015, Dr. Paul R. McHugh, the former psychiatrist-in-chief for Johns Hopkins Hospital and its current Distinguished Service Professor of Psychiatry, published a commentary in the calling it exactly what it is—a mental disorder. In this publication, he stated that "transgender surgery is not the solution for people who suffer a "disorder of 'assumption'"—the notion that their maleness or femaleness is different than what nature assigned to them biologically." ([37]) He also went on to say "that the suicide rate among transgendered people who had reassignment surgery is 20 times higher than the suicide rate among non-transgender people.

Dr. McHugh further noted studies from Vanderbilt University and London's Portman Clinic of children who had expressed transgender feelings but for whom, over time, 70%–80% 'spontaneously lost those feelings.'" ([38]). But the liberal science "experts," such as Hollywood celebrities and both the Obama and Biden administrations assert "sex reassignment" as "normal." I wonder if this is just another way the left is trying to kill people off, of depopulating the earth? The left also endorses "population control," so this would be the most logical explanation. To support this drastic response to gender dysphoria, despite what science says, is to promote death. A Dutch study, that the American Heart Association agreed with, calculated the risks of gender reassignment surgery, and showed that men taking female hormones doubled their risk of heart attack and stroke and increased their risk for blood clots by four and a half times. This same study showed that females taking male hormones tripled their heart attack risk (39). Yes, I can see how this is normal if you are a part of the liberal death cult. But the liberal elites have capitalized on the sensationalism of gender confusion and marketed dysphoria as the "right to be a victim." Confusion, deception, and lies.

The radical left's promotion of gender dysphoria has crossed from sad to sick. The transgender movement has fully infiltrated the underage arena and cross-dressing is promoted to children as "self-expression." LGBTQ parades flaunt countless little boys under twelve years old dressed in erotica and sexually posing with grown drag queens, while pedophilia in our country is out of control. But should anyone contest this abuse, they are called a "homophobe" or a "bigot." The English language has been hijacked, and words that once meant one thing have now taken on fraudulent meanings, such as "gender," "love," "hate," and "truth" to name a few; all imply new connotations which are both false and even accusatory if your reality aligns with fact, not radical fiction.

The idiocy spirals more and more out of control every day. Suddenly we're hearing reports of how being overweight isn't bad, and your doctor is "racist" if they try to convince you otherwise. This "science" entirely negates years and years of data backed by peer-reviewed studies on the dangers of obesity on one's health. We've been hearing the message about healthy diet and lifestyle since the 1980's, but suddenly liberal science puts feelings first and panders to the obese. Suddenly, a healthy diet and exercise is racist! ([39]) It has become so much easier to blame white people for not needing to lose weight than to take personal responsibility. The CDC reported that 78 percent of those who were hospitalized for Covid were considered "overweight" or "obese" ([40]). No wonder Krispy Kreme incentivized Americans to get the Covid vaccine by rewarding them with free donuts. The shameless pandering of identity politics is pathetic. One can only assume those who fall for this bull crap have never been taught critical thinking. And no, this is not an "anti-fat" tirade. This is an anti-woke tirade. The left wants all of us dead. Keeping American s fat and championing them in their fat identity keeps the Democrat votes coming in but keeps the death toll rising. That is exactly what they want.

And speaking of death, we can't finish off a chapter on the absurdity of liberal "science" without touching on abortion. The liberal death cult loves to endorse the murder of unborn children, disguising it as "women's rights" and "women's health." When young liberal men and women on various campuses are interviewed and asked the question, "When does life begin," the majority of them either refuse to answer or make up something stupid like "uhhh ... when the parents name the kid," or "when a fetus can breathe on its own." Zero science. The really weird thing is that 96 percent of biologists who are pro-choice, liberal, and non-religious agree that life begins at fertilization ([41]). These liberal scientists prove two points. Life begins at conception, and liberals have zero regard for life. The science is there, but they still condone murder. Sick assholes!

So no, liberal douchebags, we do not accept your "science" as fact. You are not the virtuous saints you advertise yourselves to be. You are a death cult, and you will be held accountable.

Conservatives love science.

CHAPTER 3

Dear Black Americans,
The Democrat party is racist. You are
being used.
Sincerely,
The past, present, and future

PLEASE PAY CLOSE attention. If you really take a hard look into the factual history of slavery in America (not the emotion-based, agenda-driven liberal fake history), you will discover that Democrats are not only the party that fought for the right to own slaves, but they founded the KKK. That's right. They founded the KKK. Even the very liberal *PolitiFact* confirms that the Democratic Party honored the first Grand Wizard of the Ku Klux Klan when he spoke at the 1868 Democratic National Convention, shortly after the Klan was founded. (40). It was founded as a political organization to intimidate Black and Republican voters in the South during reconstruction after the Civil War. According to History. com, "the KKK engaged in terrorist raids against African Americans and white Republicans at night, employing intimidation, destruction of property, assault, and murder to achieve its aims and influence upcoming elections." ([42])

Democrats have been trying to keep Black Americans in the position of "slave" to their political party and have perfected ways to make you think you want that too. It is no secret that the "War on Poverty" President Lyndon B. Johnson initiated in the 1960 s was instituted to gain the Democrat vote from minorities, especially Black minorities, in exchange for government handouts. It's called welfare. Lyndon Johnson said, "I'll have those n*ggers voting Democrat for 200 years." Of course, liberal news publications and fact checkers deny this claim, but he was a known racist, so it's really not a stretch. By labeling their policies with virtuous names like "welfare," Americans are kept under the governments control and are led to believe that those hand-outs will vanish if they don't keep voting Democrat.

It was after the "War on Poverty" was implemented that the Black nuclear family began to fall apart, and single moms and grandmas replaced the traditional nuclear family. The more children born, the bigger the check from Uncle Sam. Who needs a man in the house to bring home the bacon when the government is so graciously helping out? The more babies, the bigger the check! Incidentally, the 1960 s also happens to be when Black crime began to sky-rocket. It turns out, babies need their daddies in the home too. Don't get me wrong. There are many amazing single moms out there, who are selfless, hardworking, dedicated women making nonstop sacrifices for their babies. And those grandmas who are there to help are heroes too. I am not bashing single moms and their capabilities to raise children. Even the perfect mom cannot offer a child what the role of the father brings to the family (despite what feminists say). Even former President Barack Obama said in 2008, "Of all the rocks upon which we build our lives, we are reminded today that family is the most important. And we are called to recognize and honor how critical every father is to that foundation ... But if we are honest with ourselves, we'll admit that what too many fathers also are missing— missing from too many lives and too many homes ... You and I know how true this is in the African American commu-nity. We know that more than half of all black children live in single-parent households, a number that has doubled— doubled—since we were children ... And the foundations of our community are weaker because of it." (43) We must stop the present move to dismantle and weaken Black America!

Breitbart did an interview with Kendall Qualls, the Black leader of a Minnesota-based anti-woke movement, who said he wants to use his organization to fight against Critical Race Theory, and on to reclaim the Black nuclear family. "Qualls founded *TakeCharge* in Minnesota on Martin Luther King Jr. Day, with the goal of building a coalition of supporters in communities and in academic and business sectors 'to ignite a transformation within the Black community of the Twin Cities by embracing the core principles of America—not rejecting them.'" ([44]) This man is called an "Uncle Tom" by the racist liberals as a means of discrediting him. Somehow calling Black conservative s a racial slur is okay for these numb nuts. But Qualls is anything but an "Uncle Tom." He knows what the woke White liberals and their sheep followers are trying to do, and he is stepping up to put a stop to it.

Today's Democrat party deceives America by deflecting the responsibility for systemic racism onto "White" folks. Friends, it is not White folks causing the problem. It is the Democrat party who is fully responsible for systemic racism. Democrats unabashedly use Black Americans and any other minority party they can manipulate. They need that vote. They don't care about you. They care about power. They lie, cheat, steal, and manipulate. They point their hypocritical fingers, making false accusations that destroy lives while they are entirely guilty of these very things, if not worse. They will say and do anything to get your vote and make you believe they will change your world. But they don't care about you. You are nothing but a vote. Malcolm X said, "The worst enemy that the Negro have is this White man that runs around professing to love Negroes and calling himself a liberal, and it is following these White liberals that has perpetuated problems that Negros have. If the Negro wasn't taken, tricked, or deceived by the white liberal, then Negros would get together and solve our own problems. I only cite these things to show you that in America, the history of the White liberal has been nothing but a series of trickery designed to make Negros think that the white liberal was going to solve our problems. Our problems will never be solved by the White man." ([45]) Amen.

And so, the "White liberal savior" develops a plan that will keep the woke Black American crowd voting Democrat even longer. The White liberal savior wants to give Black American s reparations for slavery they were never personally a part of. More government handouts—of course! Sounds like a great way to keep the Black citizens down and dependent. Larry Elders from put together a short film debunking the myth that says 12.5 million Africans were "kidnapped" from their homes by White men. Through factual, historical accounts, Elders describes the active slave trade that took place in Africa long before White men set foot on the soil. These slaves were sold by their own people. He also discovered that there were more White slaves in Africa than there were sold/traded to the United States, a little fact that seems to get magically overlooked. ([46]) So perhaps Africa owes White folks' reparations for what happened back then? No? Does that sound ridiculous? It's the same stupid concept. Reparations is just more White liberal manipulation and an attempt to keep Black Americans as slaves to the Democrat party. Wake up!

Think about it. All the media talked about for months was how racist Donald Trump was. They twisted his words and slandered his character and made multiple minority groups believe he was the literal devil. But Trump's presidency brought tremendous victories for Black business owners, especially Black female business owners. He made significant increases in allocations to historical Black colleges and universities, and in 2018, brought the Black poverty level in the United States to an all-time low. And those are just a few of his pro-Black/minority moves. He appointed countless Black men and women to high positions in our government and repeatedly invited minority groups to the White House to discuss policy and change. The media did not report on this. It didn't fit their false narrative about the "racist" president. Donald Trump was never accused of these things until he swore to take down the "swamp," that is, our government. The globalist swamp fights dirty and are fighting hard to keep their hold.

This leads me to Joe Biden, the actual racist president of the U S. Are you aware of the horrific racist past of our demented Commander in Chief? This is all verifiable information with a simple internet search. Joe Biden made the following statements:

- "I tell you if you have a problem figuring out whether you're for me or Trump, then you ain't Black" (May 2020).

- "Unlike the African American community, with notable exceptions, the Latino community is an incredibly diverse community with incredibly different attitudes about different things" (2020).

- "Poor kids" just as bright as "White kids" (April 2019).

- Obama is "the first mainstream African-American who is articulate and bright and clean" (February 2007).

- "You can't go to a 7-Eleven or a Dunkin Donuts unless you have a slight Indian accent" (2006).

- "My children are going to grow up in a jungle, the jungle being a racial jungle with tensions having built so high that it is going to explode at some point" (1977, Biden made this statement to the Senate Judiciary in reference to his opposition to integration in schools. He was very pro-segregation).

Can you imagine if President Trump made any one of these ghastly statements? But if the liberal media cog is not completely ignoring these heinous remarks, they are making excuses or laughing them off as just another Biden "gaffe." OK, let's say that's true. These are just silly gaffes by this silly career politician of nearly fifty years. But when we couple the racist proclamations of Joe Biden with the racist policies he has fervently backed throughout his political pilgrimage, the evidence mounts to prove that this jackass is one of the worse racists of our time!

Biden adamantly opposed bussing minority students into "White" schools in the 1970's because he didn't want his kids learning in a "jungle." In 1977, he voted to protect the tax-exempt status of private segregated schools. It was also around this time that he repeatedly praised racial segregationists he worked with, drawing harsh criticism from many political colleagues. The cherry on top was his "1994 Crime Bill" he signed with the man-slut Bill

Clinton, leading to a significant increase of the incarceration of Black men. Yet somehow, in 2021 Biden slipped into the oval office, condemning racism and championing civil rights. He even supports Black Lives Matter! Does this not seem suspicious to you? Do you not find it awfully suspicious how Biden's greasy slimeball son Hunter flagrantly used the "N" word in his text messages, but it isn't condemned by the media? Racism is taught, my friends. He learned this from his disgusting ass-wipe parent s! Recently, the headlines read that Jill Biden said that Kamala Harris should "go f*** yourself" after Harris confronted Joe Biden on his racist past at a 2019 Democrat debate. Mrs. Biden called Harris's claim "unfounded." Wow. The blatant White privilege of these liberal degenerates is astounding. But silly Jill is a privileged Democrat who is married to racist Joe, so we must just look away.

And what about his choice for vice president? Don't you think it's suspicious that Biden chose the most unpopular and unlikeable option with a shady past and a history of racist policies? Kamala Harris is a cackling, inexperienced windbag but was chosen because she is "a woman of color." The evil Democrat overlords pushed Biden to pick her as a running mate because she had the exterior "identity" they could use to pander to Americans. They knew that they could score votes with a "female woman of color," rather than putting the most qualified person in office. They will use skin color to brownnose for votes, and there is no depth too low for them to sink to.

But, you say, certainly a president who supports the Black Lives Matter movement couldn't be racist! Guess what, honey. If they are a radical Democrat, they are racist. Black Lives Matter is an organization that chose a name targeted at drawing upon the emotions of the Black community and capitalizing on feelings of victimhood. The organization collects millions in donations with the overwhelming majority of the profit being directed to salaries, benefits, and consulting fees. In 2020, Black Lives Matter raised over 90 million dollars, and the Black communities that supported the movement saw just a fraction in return. (47) Why exactly do liberals support Black Lives Matter? How could they be racist if they support this "pro-Black" group?

I've got another surprise for you. BLM isn't a "pro-Black" group. It is a Marxist (communist) movement disguised as a pro-Black movement to gain support of citizens who have been convinced the system is rigged against them. Black Lives Matter and similar groups have received donations from the anti-American Nazi, George Soros (48). The goal of Black Lives Matter is not to make Black lives better. The goal of Black Lives Matter is to dismantle the United States of America, taking away the God-given freedom s our nation's great men and women have fought for. How do they swindle support? Why else would Soros contribute to this group with his donation disguised as funding "racial equity."

BLM uses "racism" as their platform and insist that the police should be defunded because of "systemic racism." Oh, the irony. Here we have the liberal Democrats backing the group that wants to take down the racist system that they are responsible for. (Laughs for days!) But at the heart of it, Black Lives Matter is encouraging segregation again (which White, liberal Karens love), are pushing for globalism (which

Nazi Democrats adore) and are putting the safety of Black communities in jeopardy by campaigning to defund and even abolish the police! The liberal death cults perfect plan.

Unfortunately, the corrupt media does not report on the actual number of Black deaths police are responsible for. As of this day in 2021, 457 white individuals were killed by police as opposed to 223 Black individuals. The media does not report these details. Black Lives Matter wants you to believe that "systemic racism" protects white Americans and targets Black Americans. They want to push this false racist narrative to divide our nation as a means of dismantling the system. They want to make Black American s feel like victims.

They want to keep Black American in mental and economic slavery rather than realizing that their policies are the only thing holding them back. They want to use the hate they are invoking in you to undo freedom in our country and instill globalism in its place. They want you to think that there will be a day in which you will not have to be held accountable for anything and that you are justified in opposing the law. Guess what? You are being lied to. You are being used by liberal Democrats. They hate you. They hate me. They hate America, and they hate freedom.

On June 1, 2021, Joe Biden gave yet another racist speech in Tulsa, Oklahoma. His speech was intended to commemorate a horrible attack by a White mob on a Black community in Greenwood, Oklahoma 100 years ago. One would think that our country has come far enough to understand that hate against any group is wrong. In fact, most Americans would agree with this and would condemn any acts of racism in the United States but not the "woke" Biden administration. Bumbling Biden said, "Terrorism from White supremacy is the most lethal threat to the homeland today—not ISIS, not al Qaeda, not the Taliban—White supremacists." (49) First of all, dude, you're White. You're also the leader of the free world. You are implicating yourself with this claim. Second, you have no substantial proof of this. Third, this statement is fundamentally racist. You are doing exactly what you blamed President Trump for on January 6...inciting unrest.

Finally, do you honestly think Americans believe that White supremacy is a bigger issue than ISIS,

al Qaeda", or "Taliban terrorists? Or how about China's threat of nuclear war when the U S government asked for information on the origins of the coronavirus? "White supremacy" is worse than that, Joe? It's worse than the millions and millions of dollars in damage that the violent riots of Antifa and BLM caused ruining countless small businesses owned by both minorities and White Americans? Seriously? Some of us realize you are shoving a phony narrative down the throats of the American people, but this stupidity is off the charts. Quit smoking the racist doobies with Omar, Talib, AOC, and Sharpton! Black Americans, please don't fall for the Democrats' race-baiting theatrics. It's all a hoax to get your vote. They don't and never have cared about you.

Injustice should never be condoned. Police brutality and unnecessary force that causes injury or death should not be condoned. Kneeling on someone's neck is *not* an act of justice. However, law enforcement officers, who have been thoroughly trained to justly and fairly carry out the rule of law, should have full support from local, state, and federal governments. These officers risk their lives every day to protect citizens from every race, gender, and economic status, and we should all be grateful. Consider that carjacking, armed robbery, rape, fleeing and alluding, arson, assault, battery, homicide, and so forth are all crimes that are punishable and require police involvement. The individuals guilty of these crimes, regardless of race, deserve to be caught and punished. They should not get off without paying the penalty for the infractions they have committed, regardless of their race, gender, or culture. Dismantling or abolishing the police hurts all communities and endangers all lives, especially minority lives.

Do you not find it the least bit suspicious that Black Lives Matter focuses on the myth of White supremacy, especially in law enforcement and conjures hate against the police, yet completely ignores both the perpetrators and victims of Black-on-Black crime? *CNSnews.com* recently wrote, "for Black victims of violent crime, a Department of Justice report for 2018 shows that 70.3% of their offenders were Black and 10.6% of their offenders were White. In other words, the overwhelming majority of violent crimes against Blacks are committed by other Blacks." [50] Why don't Black Lives Matter advocates advocate for the victims of Black-on-Black crime? Why doesn't the media focus on this? Why do liberals do nothing to stop the heinous homicide spree s every weekend in Baltimore and Chicago, and other Democrat-run cities? Because liberals are a death cult. They don't want to stop murder. They promote it. They want to depopulate, and they don't care if Black Americans kill each other off. That's what they want!

Black Lives Matter has teamed up with radical Democrats, and they are on a mission to destroy the nuclear family. This undertaking by the Democrats began with Lyndon B. Johnson. By destroying the nuclear family, the Black community is weakened. Black Lives Matter and the Democrats both know that when the nuclear family is gone, globalism is more easily attained. Can you see how this liberal movement is a covert endeavor to cause further damage to Black communities and cause a racial divide in our nation? Please tell me you are starting to understand how Black Americans are being used by these racist Democrat pigs?

This must be stopped. It is a power grab. It has nothing to do with justice for Black Americans.

Black Americans, please listen. Those of us who abhor liberal ideologies believe that God created everyone equal. We do not believe White man is your savior. We believe Americans from all races, cultures, and religions can join to become a strong, unstoppable nation steeped in liberty and justice for all. You must escape the liberal grip. Stop being used. You must understand that you are not a victim, unless you choose to remain hostage by these liberal demagogues. You can change your reality. Choose freedom from Democrat oppression and freedom from the white liberal savior. Choose freedom and stop voting Democrat!

Martin Luther King Jr. said, "Man must evolve for all human conflict a method which rejects revenge, aggression and retaliation. The foundation of such a method is love." Unity is the answer. Please stop voting these charlatans into office!

Unifying to become a stronger America means taking on the elite woke establishment. It means taking down the fakeness of the liberals who have been preaching a new moral code that entirely lacks morality. Do you want more proof of liberal racism? Let's talk about abortion statistics. Black Americans make up about 13 percent of the population yet are responsible for 32 percent of all abortions. Do you think it is a coincidence that most *Planned Parenthoods* have been strategically placed in minority neighborhoods? Believe it or not, 86 percent of these baby killers are within walking distance of a black or other minority community.

Margaret Sanger, the founder of *Planned Parenthood* wrote, "We don't want the word to go out that we want to exterminate the Negro population." ([51]) This friend of the Klu Klux Klan hated children and hated Black Americans. It is no surprise that she sided with far-left politics and voted with the Socialist party. Guess what? The current liberal left hates you too. Hillary Clinton said that she "admired" Margaret Sanger. She event went as far as to say, "When I think about what [Sanger] did all those years ago in Brooklyn," Clinton gushed, "I am really in awe of her. And there are a lot of lessons we that can learn from her life and the cause she launched and fought for and sacrificed so greatly." ([52]) What a demented racist witch. Abortion advocates recently denounced the words of Sanger, pretty much to cover their asses. They disguise preterm murder as "women's rights" and "pro-choice," but the only one who has no say is that little Black baby who could make a huge difference in the world. The liberal Karens want them gone.

It is up to you to create a free future for Black generations to come. The White liberal savior will make promises, backed up by globalists, such as Oprah and Obama. Don't you dare think they have your best interest at heart because they're Black! They get their cut, guaranteed—and they're not sharing it with you. Obama has been well-supported by his Nazi backer George Soros. Black globalists like Obama and Oprah don't care about you. They've built their empires right next to these White liberal morons. They'll say whatever it takes to keep you captive, as long as it keeps them rich!

Disclaimer: This chapter was not directed at *all* Black Americans. Many of you have long realized the power-hungry, unrelenting evil that the liberal Democrat party is. America is grateful for your truth seeking, your dedication to freedom, and your willingness to unify to defeat evil. We want all races to unify to make a strong, free America—unity in real love.

CHAPTER 4

Dear Teachers, Teachers Unions, and
Higher Education,
Shut up. Save your liberal Nazi and
woke activism for after-hours.
Sincerely,
Disgusted parents paying your rent

AMERICA IS SICK and tired of liberal teachers and professors taking advantage of their positions of influence and
subjecting children and young adults to political brainwashing. These prestigious institutions are producing
dozens and dozens of social justice warriors each semester
and are, thereby, losing tremendous credibility. Schools like
Harvard and Yale used to be the epitome of higher education. But today, any American with a brain cell should refuse
to send their child to any one of these elitist liberal swamps,
even if they were handed a full ride. These pompous ass
academics are presumptuously teaching their opinion as
fact. It is *corrupt*.

Our children enter college around the age of eighteen.
The part of the brain responsible for attention, self-mon-
itoring, impulse control, short-term memory, managing
emotional reactions, time management, reasoning, antic-
ipating events in the environment, planning for the future,
and adjusting complex behaviors is not fully developed and
does not fully develop until the age of twenty-five ([53]). This
part of the brain is called the prefrontal cortex. Because
this portion of the brain has not reached full maturity, it
makes this age group more prone to emotion-driven decisions and spontaneous judgment. That is why enlisting of
eighteen-year-old s is ideal for war—they don't weigh the
consequences of charging into battle. That is why car insur-
ance for individuals under twenty-five is higher because
they statistically take more driving risks and therefore are
more susceptible to accidents. The impulse-control portion of the brain has not yet matured. Why do you think
Winston Churchill said, "Any man under 30 who is not a

liberal has no heart, and any man over thirty who is not a conservative has no brains." ([54]) He was referencing the emotion-based, impulsivity of young adults. The full ability to make rational decisions on a regular basis has not fully developed. Decisions are more often based upon feeling and emotion, rather than upon logic.

It is for this very reason that schools and institutions that allow their staff and faculty to flagrantly preach political opinion as fact to these young, malleable minds is nothing short of a crime and a waste of a lot of good money. Education is meant to prepare an individual to be well-rounded member of their community and especially for their future endeavors in the working world. These arrogant liberal douche-bag professors are forsaking the whole "well-rounded instruction" component of their jobs and creating armies of radical anarchists who believe that flavor-of-the-day activism is more valuable than procuring the ability to process logical thought. The liberal agenda is being pushed on minds that are easily persuaded by impassioned causes. Your daughter enters college at eighteen, and by the time she's a junior, she insists on Mom and Dad using her correct "pronouns," or she'll be offended and call them Nazis. Your son leaves for college and when he visits you at Christmas, he expressed his shame for being White. You spent your entire life raising your children and investing all of yourself into them, and when these pretentious "educators" get ahold of them, boom—they've been poisoned by this toxic liberal ideology. Those slimy globalists got hold of your beautiful child, and they will not let go!

Why is this happening? Because these institutions are funded by liberal Democrat extremists and globalists to prepare young minds to become America-hating anarchists. This keeps the vote right where they want it—with the America-hating Democrats. The intent? For young minds to injudiciously follow radical liberal causes, disguised as "justice," ultimately paving the way for globalism. Many adolescents and young adults in America have already bought the lie. They have been fully prepared to fight for their very own freedoms to be taken away. They have been brainwashed to believe that freedom is selfish, and that capitalism is racist. They have not been taught the reality of what having no freedom looks like. But liberals are instructing these students with propaganda and positioning them for the future. President John F. Kennedy said, "Communism has never come to power in a country that was not disrupted by war or corruption, or both." The same goes for globalism. Liberals knows that if our country is weak, it is easier to break. They want to divide us in every way possible. They are actively dividing us by race, socioeconomic status, religion, social opinions, vaccination status, political beliefs, education, and neighborhoods. They are aiming for divide. They want to break us and assume total control.

Our fight for freedom must include defunding higher education. Our fight for freedom must involve de-platforming these extremists who hold positions in the education system. Our fight for freedom must include demanding that activism be removed from all levels of publicly funded instruction. Freedom of speech and freedom of thought are our all-American rights but pushing anti-American dogma in the American education arena is treason. This liberal fascism must stop.

The problem has gone farther than just higher education. The lunatic left also dominates public-school systems across the U S, and children are being brainwashed from their very start. Wen Wert writes, "schooling used to be about equipping pupils to succeed in life. These days (with very few exceptions) it is about politicizing them so that as many as possible are indoctrinated into the radical progressive left ideology, thus blighting their adult lives with discontent and grievances, mostly as result of being conditioned to view all life's setbacks as a form of 'oppression.'" (55). From Critical Race Theory being crammed down the throats of children as young as three years old, to transgender ideologies being incorporated into reading, writing, or math, American s are rapidly losing sight of what a "good" education looks like.

Teachers and school administrators are scared to death of being viewed as racist, so wokeness is incorporated into the curriculum with no fight. After all, they could lose federal funding if they don't cave to the woke mob. "The Department of Education on Monday proposed a rule that would prioritize federal funding for education groups that help schools develop and implement antiracist teaching standards. If the rule takes effect, the Office of Elementary and Secondary Education would increase grants to woke groups across the country. School districts in recent months have increased their efforts to weave critical race theory— the idea that America's political and economic systems are inherently racist—into K-12 curriculum standards. The

Education Department's proposal signals the Biden administration's support for this trend." (⁵⁶) So rather than focusing on the horrific grades being pumped out by public school students across the nation, let's turn the focus to teach our kids how to hate each other for their skin color. This anti-White, racist woke ideology is poison. It will take generations to undo. And, for the record, when the left uses "anti-racist," what they are actually saying is "anti-White." I've heard boatloads of liberal pseudo-intellectuals trying to break it down for the rest of us peasants. They often contradict each other because their agenda is based upon a "theory" that is pretty much being made up as they go. This is precisely why it is a crime to inject this dangerous philosophy into our children. It is emotion-based sewage.

And because of the phony "smart" bourgeois, woke public schools are now able to teach children that our country was founded on racism. Socialism and anti-patriotism are being pushed by teachers, and young minds are being persuaded to hate the United States. Children are being taught that Black Lives Matter isn't a political group but, rather, a "human rights" platform, and parents just sit back and ignorantly allow this indoctrination to take place. The parents who believe that these ideologies are harmless have mistaken education for brainwashing. Learning about LGBTQ in elementary school has become a priority in the public education system, as well as learning to that Whites are inherently racist and privileged. The Oregon Department of Education recently announced that math is racist and is rooted in "White supremacy," and of course the half-baked experts in California jumped on the bandwagon. (⁵⁷)

California, like other states, has come under intense scrutiny for its promotion of certain race- and ethnic-based instruction.

In March of 2021, researcher Chris Rufo highlighted California's proposed ethnic studies "model curriculum," which included, among other things, chanting the names of Aztec gods in an attempt to build unity among schoolchildren. That particular deity, Tezkatlipoka, was honored with human sacrifice. According to the World History Encyclopedia, an impersonator of Tezkatlipoka would be sacrificed with his heart removed to honor the deity. ([58]) This paganism is welcome, disguised as "cultural awareness. The lunatic left is anti-God, anti-Christ, anti-logic, anti-rationality, anti-freedom, and anti-America. If the "culture" of Christianity is not allowed in schools, the culture of pagan gods must be omitted. Parents must rise to stop this globalist brainwashing of our youth. Our children are not pawns. This is not 1940 s Nazi Germany where propaganda infiltrates curriculum and young minds are educated with propaganda, lies, and altered history.

The New York Post wrote an article in January 2021, about a married father with two children in the New York public school system who is incredibly disturbed by the anti-White, wokeness being preached to his kids in their classrooms. He feels helpless and has no idea how to combat this very serious problem. This man did not use his real name for the article for fear of retaliation upon his children or his family. ([59]) Parents around the country who feel the same frustration are afraid to speak up, but they must. This indoctrination cannot continue. Parents must be vigilant about what their children are learning and if public schools are the only option, deprogramming at home must take place on a daily basis. One or two aggressive and radicalized idiots on the school board should not be making all the decisions. How sick our world has become! We used to sit our children down and talk about "stranger danger." Now we must also talk to them about the dangers of what their activist teachers are preaching in the classroom.

This woke education system is pointing fingers at everyone else, making proclamations about who is racist and who is sexist, yet the rhetoric they preach is exactly that—racist and sexist. They are the first to call someone a "bigot," yet they are completely unwilling to hear an opposing view. They are anti-American, anti-God, and anti-freedom. We have come to the point where remaining silent against these radical leftist Nazis is not an option anymore. You must speak up on behalf of future generations. Whether it be at school functions or even with local or state representatives, your voice and our children matter—*now!* I wish I could say your vote mattered, but, in all honesty, I can't at this point. However, it is still important to try. These wicked woke liberals must be voted out. Save our children! Save our country!

CHAPTER 5

Dear feminists,
You've lost sight of reality.
Your "empowerment" makes women
look weak.
Sincerely,
Women who know that women
aren't victims

THERE IS JUST so much whining! Please stop! It's already painful having to listen to some of the crap you come up with, but you must know that you cannot speak for all women. This victim foolishness is beyond nauseating. Most feminists legitimately make women sound weak and dumb. Not all of you do, but some, especially the ones who get airtime. They make y'all look real bad. There are several problems with these windbags.

Let's start with this one. Do I really need to explain the gender pay gap thing? I feel like it is so obvious that an explanation would be superfluous. I'll keep it very brief. *Women make different choices than men do*. Allow me to dumb this down a little more. In the grand scale of life and considering the averages that take account of all women in the United States, women often choose jobs, positions, and schedules that accommodate their families. This is a choice. This does not mean that society pushed them into this because of those "evil societal norms."

This means that God put in most women the desire to care for a family, and for most women, the job comes second. I don't care if this makes your skin crawl. I don't care if this is not politically correct. I don't care if this goes against every belief in your turquoise-haired head. You can fight it all you want, but just because you chose this battle, doesn't mean it's legit. Let me say this another way. Just because your liberal arts professor insisted what they claim is "truth", doesn't mean it's true.

In this case, you lose. There may be particular instances in which your argument proves to be correct. But in the grand scale of the "gender pay gap," it all equals out. Make better choices. Work hard. And try this: be thankful for how far women have come! If you would like to have this explained to you further, please go to *PragerU.com* and search "gender wage gap." ([60]) It's really not that difficult.

Now that I've pissed off a bunch of weirdos with pink vagina hats stored away in their closets, I might as well keep going. Perhaps the most frustrating and controversial topics for anyone, regardless of where they stand on the subject is abortion. As for pro-lifers, the total and absolute neglect of "science" is what is so baffling. Ironically, science is totally disregarded in countless liberal arguments... ya, the "party of science." We often hear liberals and feminists argue that abortion is okay because they claim, "It's my body, my choice!" This is nothing short of demented. It is embarrassing that this even has to be said, but it is not technically *your* body being ripped apart and beheaded. It is not your skin being singed off in one of the most painful possible ways to die.

I recently heard Charlie Kirk, founder and president of *Turning Point USA*, give an excellent argument for this very point. A fetus's body has different DNA than its mother's body, therein proving a scientific point—it's not the mother's body that she is exterminating. It is an entirely separate human being. It is murder. That tiny little individual is a person and is alive from the time the sperm meets the egg and the DNA strands copy and divide to produce a new human entity, entirely unique from its mother. It has life, which is scientifically proven. Yet somehow there is a major disconnect on the liberal side in that argument. Here's a suggestion: It is *your right* to protect yourself from pregnancy. By doing so, you won't have to go through the trauma of an abortion and the mental anguish you are almost guaranteed to face later. That's right—they never really discuss that with you. A report in 2008 stated that PTSD rates increase by 61 percent after abortion ([61]). Choosing to kill your own baby will undoubtedly haunt you. But the idiots promoting this as "women's health" won't tell you this truth.

So, why don't pro-choice feminists care about the rights of the unborn women? Can you even imagine all of the great women who would have made tremendous positive changes to our world but who have been dismembered and destroyed at the direction of their own mother? Let's take that a step further. Can you imagine all of the great minority women? Race is such a precious topic for liberals right now, but for some reason it is entirely overlooked when we examine the abortion rates and how Black American women, specifically, have always had higher rates of abortion than any other ethnicity. Why don't feminists help women find solutions other than murder? The whole "they aren't a person yet" argument is emotion-based and lacks scientific value. Save it. Arguments like that are created to sooth the guilt of dreadful, selfish decisions. And as I touched on in the last segment, abortion is incredibly racist, targeting minorities from its very start.

Of course, there is the argument that women who have suffered rape and incest are a great reason to condone and promote abortion, yet those incidences make up less than 1 percent of the total number of abortions. ([62]) So where does that leave us? It leaves us to believe that feminists who promote abortion as a "woman's right" are promoting murder as a means of alleviating their responsibility. These individuals conceive a child, and rather than owning up to parental and societal obligations, they would rather commit murder. It's the easy, selfish way out. Commit murder but call it something else. Liberals love to give labels to things that create mythical new identities. Murder as a "women's right" is certainly one of them.

Abortion goes hand in hand with the whole globalist desire to depopulate the earth. Unfortunately, their mission has been incredibly successful. The global cabal is the death cult, so it makes sense when you look at it like that. But they seem especially eager to depopulate the Black American group. The racist liberal Democrats who hate Hispanic and Black American s target minority neighborhoods with abortion clinics disguised as a place for women's "health." Yet there is nothing healthy about ripping a developing human out of its mother's body. One will suffer an incredibly painful death, and the other will suffer immense regret or denial the rest of her life. Feel defensive about your abortion? Ya... that's all a part of the guilt.

Funny, but the *only* thing that biological women can do that biological men cannot do is have a baby. It is mind-numbing for me to think feminists, of all people, are fighting for the right to stop the only thing they can do that men cannot—giving birth to a baby! A woman, unlike a man, has the right to murder her own child, and feminists think this is okay and publicly brag that they killed their own child. Maybe it was a little girl or maybe a little boy. Regardless, it is a child who will never have a shot at making this world better. What's even funnier is that liberals claim that men can have a baby—but we have yet to see a man standing in line at the abortion clinic because they accidentally got pregnant. Science? Nope! Not an ounce.

Abortion is murder. Abortion is racist. Fight for the rights of *all* women. Vote pro-life.

Here's some advice, feminists. This comes from the *Heritage Foundation*: "Strong families remain America's best anti-poverty, anti-crime, pro-health, pro-prosperity institution. Rather than denigrating the role of motherhood, let's celebrate it as one of the most noble choices a woman can make." ([63])

Why is science such an obstacle for liberal feminists? It is for liberals in general, but this particular issue brings incredible hypocrisy and contradiction. I can't say all feminists are behind this one, but transgenderism must really make some of you uncomfortable. Some of you support the rights of women, yet those liberal idiots you voted in are pushing for transgenders (or biological men) to compete against biological women. Where do you fall on this? How can you possibly be okay with this? What about men (oops, I meant transgenders) in the ladies' restroom or fitting room? Do you think it's okay for a woman who has been raped or assaulted to be forced to share a restroom with an enormous male because he identifies as "Tina"? *What about biological women's rights?*

The inconsistencies are endless. At some point, it's time to make an ethical choice, not based upon political party, not based on feelings, but rather on what is best for all (actual) women (born with ovaries, a uterus, and a vagina).

Policies are being written that harm biological women. What is wrong with you?

The "Me Too" movement is a great example of feminist inconsistencies. This organization offers a voice for victims of sexual crime and endeavors to help victims of rape, sexual assault, and unwanted sexual advancements. The movement gained attention a few years ago after multiple celebrities outed the famed pervert Harvey Weinstein for the heinous sexual crimes he had committed against them. The phrase "believe all women" was heard everywhere, and those who were plagued with the trauma of rape finally felt they had been given a voice to point a finger at their violator. However, this seemingly virtuous revolution quickly become politicized. Crying "me too" was weaponized when President Trump appointed a right-leaning judge to the Supreme Court. Judge Kavanaugh's life was scrutinized and picked apart to an extreme, and his charlatan liberal accuser shamelessly fabricated the sketchiest of stories with zero accountability and absence of any proof. But the liberal army of freaks hated Trump's choice because they hated Trump. They would have done anything to keep his choice out of the Supreme Court.

Of course, the feminists screaming "believe all women" weren't anywhere to be found when Joe Biden's accuser, Tara Reide, came forth, yet again declaring that she was sexually assaulted by then Senator Biden, in 1993. This "me too" didn't work for the liberal agenda, so they didn't care. And naturally the mainstream media puppets unleashed havoc on Tara Reide's reputation, doing everything in their power to discredit her allegations and her character. Feminist hypocrisy is disgusting.

I am all for women's rights when it doesn't push the boundaries of science, common sense, or truth. The fact that so many feminists are man-haters yet sit silent when a full-blown dude with a penis and the family jewels says he feels like a lady and dominates a woman's sport. How does your brain make this okay? How are you okay with a biological male competing in the female MMA arena and crushing his biological female opponent's skull? (⁶⁴) How are you okay with biological males stealing medals from biological females that have trained their whole lives to compete against other biological women, only to have their victory ripped away? Why are men being allowed to take more from women; isn't this precisely what you are fighting against? This all makes feminists look like dicks.

Disclaimer: I am truly sorry if you are the victim of rape, assault, incest, or any other form of invasion against your will. That is wrong, that is horrible, and I hope the aggressor who harmed you is punished to the highest letter of the law. I sincerely hope you have found the resources that you need to help you through all the facets of life that have been affected by this trauma. If you have not sought help, please do. There are countless resources waiting to help you through. There are countless people praying for you; I can guarantee that. Please know that you are never alone.

CHAPTER 6

Dear White liberals,
You are phony. Your wokeness is
hypocritical and disingenuous.
You are racist.
Sincerely,
Everyone that knows your "Black Lives
Matter" lawn sign is a decoy
because you're afraid of Black people

THERE IS JUST so much red meat here, it's hard to know where to start. Over the last few years, White liberals have metamorphosed from extremely obnoxious, ignorant, and pretentious morons into the absolute epitome of racist hypocritical bigot douche bags. These charlatans bow down and kiss anyone's ass that isn't White. However, if you are a White Democrat politician or White liberal celebrity, you are exempt from being called a racist, despite how low you go. Example? Well, we've already touched on the deep racist roots of "big guy" Joe Biden. But how about his son who Biden called "the smartest guy I know." If you've ever heard the adage that "racism is taught," here is the perfect go-to example. Man-slut, crackhead, and pedophile Hunter Biden happens to be a chip off the old block. *Wire Daily News* wrote, "Hunter Biden used anti-Black racial slurs and accidentally sent an explicit picture when texting with his attorney in 2018, according to a report, and the news comes just a week after his father decried racism while speaking in Tulsa, Oklahoma." (⁶⁵) Did the mainstream media propagandists cover this? Nope! They let it slide. Why? Because their fake "wokeness" is a cover for their deep-seated racism. And since they're Democrats, there's nothing to see here!

Over and over again, we are hearing some of the most vocal "woke" Democrats and Trump-haters outed for their disgusting racist comments. Billie Eilish was recently called out for racist slurs against Asians she made, but in defense she stated, "I'm being labeled something that I am not." (⁶⁶) Doesn't feel very good, does it Billie? White American s are being called racist for doing absolutely nothing but existing. We are the ones who get to say, "I'm being labeled something that I am not." You, however, are a racist liberal loser, and we have proof!

The Blaze recently wrote, "Ultra-woke soccer star Megan Rapinoe—who once gave a speech saying, "This is my charge to everyone: We have to be better ..." and has virtue-signaled around the globe for progressive causes such as lack of diversity and the evils of White supremacy and former President Donald Trump—actually may be in trouble with cancel culture" ([67]). This dumbass made a racist tweet against an Asian individual. But this woke hypocrite is in good company with the rest of the White liberal hypocrites. All are racist!

But somehow the wokeness of liberal Democrats functions like armor that fends off any facts or truth that may hold their bigotry accountable. Critical thinking isn't even on the table with these die-hard bootlickers. If their cause creates division, is evil, morally bankrupt, or anti-American, White libs are all for it. The double standard is astounding. But when your soul is as black as the black-face costume you sported at Halloween a few years ago (Joy Behar), and you happen to be an obnoxious loudmouthed lib, then you are exempt from being labeled "racist."

The White liberals that think they are somehow making a difference with their "Black Lives Matter" sign in the yard and condemning other White people for being "privileged" truly are the worst. You are the biggest Karen s of them all. You are hiding your hate behind your yard sign. "Please don't come on my property, angry Black people! I'm on your side! My best friend is Black!" The sleaziness of these pricks is off the charts. Here's some news for you prejudiced hypocrites, all of God's creation have been created equal. All of us. I'm not kissing anyone's ass because of their skin color, and I don't expect my ass to be kissed by anyone. And I'm certainly not going to kiss someone's ass just to keep them off of my lawn. *Your White savior complex is racist.*

Critical Race Theory does nothing but further segregate America and force a narrow-minded hate-based divide. At the very root of the dogma, Critical Race Theory is racist in and of itself. Anyone who denies this, regardless of the color of their skin, is both ignorant and *privileged.* This malignant doctrine is being taught as an absolute, and brainless libs are gobbling it up, but mostly just to virtue signal their fellow American s and parade their phony morality. These racist teachings go directly against what the Civil Rights movement of the 1960 s was all about and seek to demolish the work of the anti-segregationists who made enormous strides for racial equality. The "systemic" problems that exist in the United States have been meticulously crafted by the Democrat party. The lies, the abuse of power, and the unconscionable failure to actually help Americans in need, especially minorities, has been the liberal Democrat way for over a hundred years.

Lies are told to Black Americans that "Republicans are racist" and that "Republicans only want to promote those that are wealthy or White." These lies are proliferated by the racist media cyborgs and circulated to the public. Con artists, disguised as politicians, pander to minority groups, and these deceptions garner votes. Which party is so focused on skin color? *Democrats.* The goal? Total control. The last page? Globalism. The price? Everything you ever hoped for. Freedom.

Dumb White liberals are so focused on trying to act as a White savior to Black Americans that it seems they are in some sort of fake hero fog and can't recognize the actual damage they are doing. They are being brainwashed and used as drudges. They have bought into the anti-American, anti-law enforcement, anti-peace, and anti-freedom mentality their radicalized representatives have been selling to them. But their wokeness is harming everyone, especially Black Americans and all other minority groups. Being woke is being racist, and it doesn't matter what color your skin is.

The extremist views that are being shoved down the throats of innocent Americans, including naïve children, are both foul and agenda driven. They are aimed at indoctrinating the masses to procure a majority of dumbasses who don't ask questions. "White privilege" is a perfect example. It is hard to believe this bizarre, even comical concept is even a thing. Making sweeping statements about an entire race is the way the Nazi party worked. The propaganda pushed by the media, social media, higher education, and politicians in this absurd movement makes Hitler look like an amateur. The goal? Again—power.

Americans are being turned against each other by the anti-American global cabal disguised as Democrat politicians. They want total control, and you idiot libs are the henchmen carrying out the evil deeds. Just a few years ago, Martin Luther King Jr. was praised by White liberals. If he were alive today, they'd call him an Uncle Tom, just like they call any other Black American who disagrees with their liberal propaganda. Have you heard how they talked about Larry Elder as he ran for governor of California? They called this Black conservative a "White supremacist". How do these asshats not realize the racist hypocrisy? Liberalism generates leftist Nazis and herd mentality. It overtakes logic, kindness, compassion, scientific thought, goodwill, equality, honesty, and integrity. These virtues are replaced by neo-totalitarian principles being pushed by bullying, virtue-signaling, slander, censorship, and hate. This is the Democrat party, the racist party of hate, also known as a radicalized liberal death cult.

I saw a quote on *Instagram* from a blogger by the name of Matt Walsh who said, "I've been fascinated to learn that only White people have ancestors who did bad things. Slavery, conquest, rape, etc. Only White people. We're the only ones who have to apologize. No one else. Everyone else is descended from angels. Really mind-blowing news. I had no idea." This man sums up the stupidity of White liberals who pretend to buy into this obnoxious movement. Ya...White people are the only bad guys. That must be why other countries that are not predominantly White are utopias, right? *Please.*

One of the most pathetic stories to hit the headlines recently is that Washington state Governor Inslee, along with other governors throughout the U S, are making Critical Race Theory training a requirement for public school teachers. Inslee writes, "The legislature plans to continue the important work of dismantling institutional racism in public schools and recognizes the importance of increasing equity, diversity, inclusion, antiracism, and cultural competency training throughout the entire public school system." ([68]). Nothing herald s stupidity more than this obnoxious White savior's proclamation. Nothing proves more that White liberals are pushing full-blown racism under an "anti-racism" guise. This bill violates many Civil Rights laws that were signed into effect in the 1960 s, and prominent Black, Hispanic, and Jewish leaders are speaking out against this racial curriculum, condemning it as harmful to children. But the White liberal saviors must insist that they will fix it all, never mind what those minorities have to say. Governor Inslee is a White racist scumbag and is only following the lead of the weak idiot, Joe Biden. On Biden's very first day in the oval office, he rescinded the Trump administration's executive order prohibiting Critical Race Theory training for federal agencies and federal contrac-tors ([69]). As stated earlier, Joe Biden is and always has been very vocally racist against many minority groups. His push to promote Critical Race Theory is a push to segregate our country racially once again and to weaken us as a nation. The weaker we are as a people, the easier we are to control. What do you get when you cross zero morals, zero ethics, and racism? A White liberal. When we multiply "White lib-eral" with mob mentality, we get leftist Nazi extremists with anti-American rhetoric and nothing but the destruction of freedom in mind.

Here's a perfect, small-scale example of a "rescue" by an everyday White liberal savior. A White male deputy pulled over a car for having no license plate. He did not know who was inside the vehicle. When he approached, he found a Black female driver and a Black male passenger. The

Black female driver did not have her license and claimed that the male passenger was teaching her how to drive. Unfortunately, the male passenger also did not have a driver's license. The deputy had to ask the individuals to step out of the car, as neither of them were licensed to operate a vehicle. The individuals, while annoyed, were very cooperative and allowed the deputy to process the citation while they arranged for a ride home.

Meanwhile, a morbidly obese White woman inserting herself into a situation that is entirely unrelated to her is not White supremacy? But this pasty-white marshmallow actually thought she was able to save these more-than-capable Black people. How disgusting. How *racist*.

A grand scale example of a White liberal savior is Joe Biden's claim that voter I.D. is racist. How can Democrats keep a straight face? While we all know that Biden and his demonic Democrat cohorts are desperately trying to keep voter I.D. out of the picture so that they can scam the elections by millions like they did in 2020. They stare directly into the camera and claim to the public that requiring an I.D. for American s is racist. Liberal Democrats love to tell the American people that we should be like Europe but remain completely silent about the fact that forty-six out of forty-seven European countries require voter I.D. ([70])

Perhaps we should break this down. An I.D. is required to drive, to fly, to buy a house, to get a formal education, to open a bank account, to buy alcohol, to buy cigarettes, to apply for welfare, to apply for food stamps, to apply for Medicare/Social Security, to apply for a job or to apply for unemployment, to rent or buy a car, to get married, to legally purchase a gun, to adopt a pet, to rent a hotel room, to apply for a hunting or fishing license, to buy a cell phone, to visit a casino, to make a blood donation, and to purchase certain cold medications, to name a few ([71]). But Biden, who thinks that minorities are too stupid to know how to operate a computer or to get a lawyer or accountant to run a business, also thinks minorities are incapable of getting an I.D. to use for voting. What could possibly be more racist? Oh, I know: actual Jim Crow laws. Those laws are actually racist. Yet numbskull Biden tries to say voter I.D. is *worse* than Jim Crow laws.

Honestly, how can any single American take this B.S. serious? Yet in his flowing cape, the great White liberal savior Biden, acting as a defender of those poor, helpless minorities, is flagrantly working to keep illegal votes skyrocketing in favor of the Democratic ballot. That is shameless racism, gaslighting anyone who gets in the way. White liberal politicians are absent of anything that is virtuous or good. They are entirely void of God and, to put it plainly, are bound for hell.

While Democrats scream that voter I.D. is racist, they strongly push for vaccine passports for all Americans. How is this not pure hypocrisy? It's sick!

Thomas Sowell said, "Racism is not dead, but is on life support—kept alive by politicians, race hustlers, and people who get a sense of superiority by denouncing others as "racists" ([72]). The phoniness of White liberals and their self-righteous hypocrisy is enough to make most patriots heave. These far-left extremists are infiltrating every walk of life and undoing the incredible progress in race relations that have evolved since the Civil Rights Movement. We must stop these liberal Democrat extremists from stealing our freedom. Wokeness is weakness. Unity is the only answer.

CHAPTER 7

Dear liberal men,
Masculinity isn't toxic and you're a
bunch of pansy-ass wimps.
Sincerely,
Real women who know masculinity
is hot, and real men who want to
beat your ass

THIS TOPIC IS simultaneously both comical and sad. Somehow, men (and yes, this means individuals born with a penis and testicles) have been convinced by deranged liberals that masculinity is harmful. Liberals, who use identity politics to wage their war on every single aspect of our lives, have decided that if you are a masculine male, you are toxic. They have even managed to link the idea of masculinity with being a "Trump supporter," which screws with the minds of weakling liberal males who don't know their elbow from their asshole. Because they so desperately don't want to be confused as a conservative or a Republican, they go out of their way to achieve a touch of femininity. Most of these males are straight yet strive for dab of girliness. Oh, they will most definitely have a beard; don't let that fool you. That is part of the liberal male feminine dress code, along with a man-bun and tattoos (flannel shirt optional). But they shun actual manliness and cling to any and everything that makes up the liberal male formula. These weak minded, weak-bodied man-boys are sometimes called "soy boys" after a study claimed that consumption of too much soy increased estrogen in men. ([73])

While soy-induced femininity may or may not be true, it is clear that liberals are using a scalpel to separate the masculinity from the man and will say whatever it takes to get the job done. Condemning meat-eating is one approach. It's hard to find a vegan or vegetarian man whose girlfriend didn't convince him to trade in his prime rib for an "Impossible Burger". These men live with their testicles in a vice 24/7. They have been convinced by the media, by the education system, and by society that to be a "real man" is toxic, and therefore, they must surrender who they really are to appease everyone else. What a joke.

Liberal men, it is time to grow a pair. You are being used by the liberal left to undo society, and when American society comes undone, freedom is gone. And that means everyone's freedom, not just people the liberals disagree with. And no, it won't be a glorious utopia where everyone is equal, and we all have the same benefits. That is the globalist lie regurgitated to the masses by idiots like Bernie Sanders and AOC. The global cabal wants full control of your life in every single aspect, and they are masterfully convincing you that this is what you want too.

When you give up your masculine identity and succumb to the anti-male and anti-nuclear family dogma, you are surrendering control to the liberal elite. They hate the idea of you having your own identity. They hate the concept of free thought. The liberal left is instructing gullible, spineless men on what their "new" identity should be. That is why the media slams men for being manly and why entertainment is demasculinizing. They are skillfully redesigning our culture to be weak, unpatriotic, and unwilling to see their "truth" from reality. They want you to hate America and are trying to convince you that being American is racist and that you're a dumb redneck if you love your country. If you have bought into this jackass jargon, you have gone way past dumb, and your critical thinking skills mega suck. If you admire Don Lemon, Anderson Cooper, or Fredo (aka Chris Cuomo) as being smart, good examples of what a man is, you have succumbed to a full brainwashing, and you must be deprogrammed. But also, if you have deliberately feminized yourself in any way, just to be distanced from being identi-fied as "conservative," you are a coward. Weak. A beta.

What young liberal men today do not understand is what bravery is. Bravery is volunteering to leave the com-forts of your life only to be sent into the trenches where you may lose everything for the cause of freedom. Young men used to lie about their age so they could go off to war and fight for their country. Today, cartoons hurt their feel-ings, and mean words send them into the corner to curl up in fetal position and cry like a newborn baby. If there is any "privilege" in our society today, it is the liberal priv-ilege that adolescent and young adults are being taught by the liberal elite to hate capitalism, to hate patriotism, and to hate America. They use their First Amendment right to shred and dismantle the historical foundations of our nation. They want to destroy what millions of brave men and women have died for. These privileged liberal youth are shockingly ignorant to the factual history or our country and rally to destroy the bedrock of the greatest nation on earth. Why? Because they are being used by the radicalized liberal elites to take down America. They are being used to destroy their own freedom. They are emptyheaded, ignorant sheep that have been programmed to destroy themselves, their country, and their own liberty. And with their undeveloped prefrontal cortex, they don't even realize it's happening.

The liberal globalist establishment has infiltrated the American military with the intent of making our country look weak to our adversaries around the world. A recent ad campaign for army recruitment triggered such a fury from American patriots that the army turned off the "comment" section on their ad page. The commercial was an ad that pandered the "woke" and made the American military look like a body of gay activists. ([74]) Way off mark!

Meanwhile, Putin's army generates ads for military recruitment that strike fear into viewers around the world. ([75]) *This is what a military should look like.* Tough. Mean. Ready for attack. And yes—*masculine.* I can't believe how many American veterans are mortified by this shameful and embarrassing campaign. It is *the worst!* The military must be tough, and masculinity is required. This is not to say that women should not take part in our military forces. They absolutely should. But gender identity and sexual preference is the last thing our military should be promoting. This wokeness is weakness, not progress. This is a joke, and it should infuriate every man and woman in America, regardless of how soft you are.

Recently *The New York Post* published an article about the wokeness in our military. "Republican lawmakers, Arkansas Sen. Tom Cotton and Texas Rep. Dan Crenshaw, launched a campaign urging whistleblowers in the armed forces to expose progressive diversity training programs, some of which have reportedly deemed White people 'inherently evil.'" ([76]) "The effort followed Cotton's Thursday meeting with Lt. Col. Matthew Lohmeier, the former Space Force commander who was relieved of his duties after claiming that Marxism is invading the military through diversity, inclusion and equity training courses required by higher-ups in the Pentagon." (77). This effort to make our military less "masculine" is an effort by the globalists to take down America. This is a Marxist effort with globalism as the intended end result.

Making our military weak leaves the U S vulnerable and a laughingstock to the world. The military is the last place for wokeness. This should alarm every single American.

Our enemies see this weakness. Jinping, Putin, Kim Jong-Un, and the Taliban are laughing their assess off at the fragile state of our nation and the pathetic level-ten weakness of the Biden administration. They are licking their chops. President Trump had the balls to command respect and orchestrate progress with our global adversaries. And "balls" are needed for some things, you wussy liberal invertebrates! Grow a pair!

It goes without saying, but I'll say it anyway. Biden is one of the best examples of a weak male there is. He is the biggest coward our nation has ever seen in the highest office, and he will face God for his crimes against not only the American people, but the Cuban people and the Afghan people. If he stays in his current position, that list is guaranteed to grow. He is disgusting in every way. Vile. Sick. Sinful. Soulless. This sorry excuse for a leader, a human, a male... must be impeached, along with his entire sorry ass administration. Joe Biden is a liar, a thief, a pedophile, a traitor, a rapist, a racist, and a globalist, and his totalitarian rule should make every American's blood boil! Our great nation deserves better.

CHAPTER 8

Dear World,
There is an answer to your problems.
Sincerely,
Love

On the World

THERE IS ONE answer to the nightmare that is liberalism. It also happens to be the answer to hate, racism, segregation, hypocrisy, dishonesty, and every other unethical and immoral problem within humanity. The irony is that it is the last thing in the world that any liberal leftist would look to for answers—and not just liberals. Any and every single human being on this planet, who is lost, empty, or confused, is being offered a solution.

There has been a war on anything that has to do with the Bible, God, Jesus, Christians, or even faith for the last 2,000 years. You see, "liberalism" did not just form over the course of the last century. It is an anti-God, anti-Christ mind-set that our planet is fully entrenched in, and it is only getting worse. The Bible says in Ephesians 6:12, "For we wrestle not against flesh and blood, but against principalities, against powers, against the rulers of the darkness of this world, against spiritual wickedness in high places." The effects of this evil are manifested as hate, murder, lust, greed, envy, gluttony, dishonesty, and laziness. It is racism, abortion, and confusion about personal identity. This unholy hell is being unleashed upon the world and touted as virtue. Those who insist upon cramming this wickedness down the throats of the rest of the us gaslight, mock, ridicule, and falsely accuse anyone who doesn't join in. They call us "haters" and "racist" for not bowing to Critical Race Theory. They call men "misogynists" if they don't want to date a transvestite, and Nazis if you have American pride. It is endless! Up is down;

down is up. There is no moral compass in the woke society. It is a depraved free-for-all.

The Bible says in 1 Corinthians 1:18, "For the message of the cross is foolishness [absurd and illogical] to those who are perishing *and* spiritually dead [because they reject it], but to us who are being saved [by God's grace] it is [the manifestation of] the power of God." In other words, if a person doesn't believe that Jesus died on the cross for their sins, they are spiritually dead. They cannot comprehend the love of God because they choose to reject it. There is a spiritual war in our world. Those who do not understand the tenets of the Gospel are confused when Christians don't agree with their secular ideologies, and Christians are ridiculed for not jumping on the woke bandwagon. I can't tell you how many times I've heard a self-proclaimed atheist say don't believe in the "big man in the sky." It's like they all got this line from the "I'm a fool" playbook. The world does not understand the reality of the spiritual situation we live in and why Christians will not comply. This infuriates the pagan Democrat morons and exactly why there is a war on free speech, on religious freedom, and on our Constitution. They cannot control Christians. Christians will not give in. We answer to a higher power. We answer to God, and we will bow to no one else.

On Race

God has made it very clear that He created man equal. He has no favorite race or skin color. The Bible says in Acts 17:25 – 28 that "God made all races and nations, all of us by one blood (verse 26) for His purposes." We are equal. We all have the same blood. Those who understand this know that racism isn't an option. That is why we must all reject the racist programming of our children with the Critical Race Theory. We must not cave to the demands of the "woke." Thomas Sowell said, "Our children and grandchildren may yet curse the day we began hyping race and ethnicity. There are countries where that has led to slaughters in the streets, but you cannot name a country where it has led to greater harmony." ([77]) Bowing to the lefts programming and indoctrination is assisting the annihilation of freedom in this country. We must stand for equality of all races. God sent His only Son to die for *all* men and women. Every single one. There is no separation in His eyes. He loves us all just as we all must love one another as equals.

On Womanhood

Women were created beautiful. We reflect God's glory. The liberal agenda is anti-femininity and anti-beauty for females and is against men, especially heterosexual men. They have set out to destroy the fundamental reality of what it is to be a woman. They want you to kill that child inside of your womb. They want you to hate straight men and anything that has to do with the nuclear family. They want you to be an ugly, mindless sheep that fight to undo the simplicity of what God created. Liberals hate God. But they also hate you.

For these liberal demagogue's, it isn't about "women's rights"; it's about controlling women. It's about stripping your identity as a female away, dumbing you down into a woke activist, and feeding you ideologies. They don't want you to be female or males to be male. They don't want you to think for yourself and have devised a program for you to follow that discredit s actual science and panders to emotion. They tell you it's okay to make up your gender. It's okay to accuse anyone who doesn't understand your feelings of traumatizing you. They want women to be victims. They want you to be a prisoner of your own mind. This is how they trap you into conforming. They disguise it as "non-conformity," but you are doing exactly what they want. They want to break you. They want to control you. Don't be stupid enough to let them have your mind. Break free from their control.

Freedom for women comes when you break free from the captive thinking of the liberal left. If the way you used to think goes against the indoctrination you've succumbed to, it's time to break free. God made us each to be unique individuals, but that doesn't mean we need to defy nature. He wants to heal your past and heal your wounds. He wants to be in your life today. He is earnestly pursuing you and loves you like crazy, even while you are actively pushing Him away. True freedom for everyone comes from Christ and His death on the cross. His sacrifice brings liberty from the oppression of this world. He did it for you and He thinks you are beautiful.

On Manhood

Well, what does it mean to be a "real man"? This paragraph is sure to make the liberal heads spin like Linda Blair's! There is no better place to look for the example of what a "real man" is than to Jesus Christ Himself. He was not the wimpy, pasty-faced weakling that religious artists have painted Him out to be. You cannot be fully man, and fully Creator of the universe and be a featherweight pushover. Jesus's integrity, passion, penchant for action, grace, wisdom, willingness to speak openly (even offensively if necessary), self-sacrificing service, and lifetime focus on making the world better are just a few of the qualities that make Jesus the ideal standard of manhood. He is the ideal mold from which men were meant to be cast ([78]). He is a gentleman, compassionate, a servant, and a warrior all at once. He is the ultimate in humility. He is love.

So, to be a real man is to be like Jesus, who is not feminine, not a pushover, not a meathead, and not mean, abusive, or corrupt. A real man strives to be like the Creator. There is no greater example of a man than Him.

Perfection is unattainable. Jesus knows that. The old saying "not perfect, just forgiven" is true. Nothing is more manly than humility. Humility is derived from an inner strength that not many can achieve. Humbling yourself and acknowledging that you are lost is a monumental step in finding spiritual freedom. God's Son, Creator of the universe, humbled Himself and became a man, and then took the sin of the world upon Himself and died so that you could be free. He is the greatest example of humility in the history of time.

You don't have to be weak. You don't have to be a meathead. Hey, you don't even have to give up soy. And you certainly don't have to surrender manliness. You don't even have to accept Jesus. He made it a choice. But if you do choose Him, He will save you from yourself and from hell, and you will enjoy true freedom forever. The decision to be a real man is up to you.

Sincerely,
A Conservative Commoner

Post Script

AS OUR NATION is literally on the precipice of losing everything that millions of men and women have fought and died for, it is crucial that We the People rise and unite against the raging hate of the liberal left. The color of our skin, the neighborhood we live in, the level of our education, and our socioeconomic status mean nothing in the end. The Preamble to the Declaration of Independence written by Thomas Jefferson states, "We hold these truths to be self-evident, that all men are created equal, that they are endowed by their Creator with certain unalienable Rights, that among these are Life, Liberty and the pursuit of Happiness." Abraham Lincoln called this document "a rebuke and a stumbling-block to tyranny and oppression" ([79]). That includes the present-day tyranny and domination of lunatic woke politics and the global cabal.

Our country was founded upon principles of freedom from oppression and government control. We must not allow the liberal radical terrorists to rewrite history and frame our founding fathers as racists. We must not allow Democrats to deflect the responsibility of their own roots in slavery onto innocent Americans today. The White liberal saviors must be punished for their extreme racist discourse and crimes against humanity. Liberal radicals must be held accountable for the deceiving the masses with their filthy propaganda. The lies and hate of this death cult must stop.

How do we stop this anti-American mob when they steal elections and dox anyone who objects to their leftist Nazi dogma? Censorship is on the rise, and free thinkers are being blackballed. Until now, many Americans have felt a certain sense of security because our nation was founded upon Godly principles. It seemed impossible that God would desert the U S with so many of His people praying for our country while living within its boundaries. But what happens when our country deserts God? The globalists ripped Him out of schools, and Christian assembly on many campuses is forbidden. The liberal death cult condones the killing of millions of unborn babies (and even some after they are born) in the name of "woman's rights." Murder is a regular thing. Rape, pedophilia, theft—the list is endless. But then again, the Bible said this would all happen.

The world and its anti-God, hateful discourse has been condemning Christianity since AD 33, and there has been a war on the "God of Israel" since the dawn of time. The Gospel, with a message of true love, is twisted and mangled into hate because it will not conform to the sin of man, nor will it conform to anyone's "feelings." Mankind must understand and admit that he or she is wrong for the power of the Gospel to begin in their life. Men and women are sinful by nature. A sinful life is easy, and giving it up requires humility, sacrifice, and a willingness to change. Arrogance has caused mankind to elevate himself above God, only to guarantee them a place in hell. But there is hope. Even though we are all incredibly hideous inside, Jesus Christ is willing to forgive the disgusting, sick, vile, hateful, immorality of us all. He is willing to forgive the most unforgiveable. When He died, He literally took the sin of mankind upon Himself. He became sin for us. There's a lot more to this, including kicking Satan's ass, but regardless, He did it for you.

And after being dead for three days and defeating Satan, Jesus came back to life. That means He is alive right now. Literally. *He is alive!*

This serves as a warning to the lying, corrupt leaders of the world and to anyone else who thinks being a "good person" is their ticket to heaven, the Warrior King is coming back soon. You are either for Him or against Him, and He knows where you stand. What you theorize, postulate, or joke about on this subject makes absolutely no difference. The Bible says in Philippians 2:10–11 "that at the name of Jesus every knee will bow, of those in heaven, and of those on earth, and of those under the earth, and *that* every tongue will confess that Jesus Christ *is* Lord, to the glory of God the Father." That means *everyone* will bow, including George Soros, the Obamas, the Clintons, the Biden family, Adolf Hitler, Osama Bin Laden, Nero, the Taliban, and every other evil villain the world has ever known. This also includes the nicest people you know who are philanthropists, volunteers, and do-gooders at every turn. And this includes you. We all have a choice: to accept Jesus before we die or before He comes back or wait until the choice is gone. Millions will beg and plead for His forgiveness, and His response will be "Depart from me, I never knew you" (Matt. 7:23). The only option then is hell. And no, it will not be a party. You will burn. "But as for the cowardly, the faithless, the detestable, as for murderers, the sexually immoral, sorcerers, idolaters, and all liars, their portion will be in the lake that burns with fire and sulfur, which is the second death" (Rev. 21:8).

It is agonizing to write these words because I know many readers will disregard this message or laugh it off. Yes, I have complete and utter disdain for the anti-God hate of the global cabal. This book is filled with words assaulting the ideologies of the radicalized liberal left, and I understand that I wasn't "nice" in doing so. It was harsh and probably offended a big chunk of society, but I don't care if it did. The truth hurts. I don't lie. I don't pander. And I don't kiss ass. This book is not filled with gaslighting or hate. I don't care if this book hurt your feelings, and I'm not going to candy coat the facts to make one or two subgroups happy.

Where you spend eternity is up to you. I'm far from perfect but I know that my future is secure. What about you? This is the truth: Christ's return is near. Your race, culture, gender, political affiliation, or religion does not matter to Christ Jesus. He died for everyone. But you have to choose Him to be saved from hell.

You now have the information. You are responsible for what you do with it. You cannot say you didn't know.

Choose eternal freedom. Choose true Love. Choose enduring unity. Choose forgiveness.

Choose Jesus Christ.

Endnotes

1   Title: "NBA Regular Season Ratings Down Double Digits Heading into Final Week of Season"
    Author: Quentin Blount
    Title of Publication: Outsider
    Date: May 10, 2021
    Url: https://outsider.com/news/sports/nba-regular-season-rat-ings-down-double-digits-heading-final-week-season/
    Date accessed: June 3, 2021

2   Title: "George Soros: A truly evil man"
    Author: George Lombardi
    Date: July 8, 2020
    Title of Publication: George Lombardi Blog
    Url: https://www.georgeguidolombardi.com/george-soros-a-truly-evil-man/
    Date retrieved: June 8, 2021

3   Title: "New Project Veritas Video Exposes CNN Director Admitting 'Propaganda' Operation to Oust Trump"
    Author: Tristan Justice
    Date: April 8, 2021
    Title of Publication: The Federalist
    Url: https://thefederalist.com/2021/04/14/new-project-veri-tas-video-exposes-cnn-director-admitting-propaganda-opera-tion-to-oust-trump/

Date retrieved: June 8, 2021

4   Title: "Statements by Hitler and Senior Nazis Concerning Jews and Judaism"
Author: D. Irving
Book: *The War Path: Hitler's Germany 1933-1939*
Publisher: Pan Macmillan
Publisher location: ?
Date: July 14, 1983
Url: https://phdn.org/archives/www.ess.uwe.ac.uk/genocide/ statements.htm
Date retrieved: June 3, 2021

5   Title: "Why Liberals Are Anti-Semitic: Dems have become the party of Jew haters"
Author: Jeffrey Kuhner
Date: May 18, 2021
Title of Publication: Kuhner's Columns
Url: https://wrko.iheart.com/featured/kuhners-corner/con-tent/2021-05-18-why-liberals-are-anti-semitic-dems-have-be-come-the-party-of-jew-haters/
Date retrieved: June 6, 2021

6   Title: "Leftist Legislators Launch Anti-Israel Tirades On Twitter As Hamas Bombs Jewish Cities"
Author: Jordan Davidson
Date: May 13, 2021
Title of Publication: The Federalist
Url: https://thefederalist.com/2021/05/13/leftist-legislators-launch-anti-israel-tirades-on-twitter-as-hamas-bombs-jew-ish-cities/
Date retrieved: May 31, 2021

7   Title: "The rise of antisemitism on the Left and in America"- opinion
Author: Matthew Wearp
Date: July 31, 2020
Title of Publication: The Jerusalem Post

Url: https://www.jpost.com/opinion/
the-rise-of-antisemitism-in-the-left-and-in-america-637017
Date retrieved: June 3, 2020

8   Title: U.S. "moving into a dangerous phase" as anti-Semitic inci-
dents surge, group says"
Author: Unknown
Date: January 26, 2021
Title of Publication: CBS News
Url: https://www.cbsnews.com/news/
anti-semitic-incidents-on-rise/
Date retrieved: June 3, 2020

9   Title: "Biden authorized $235 million in funding to Palestinians
one month before Hamas' attacks on Israel"
Author: Libby Emmons
Date: May 12, 2021
Title of Publication: The Post Millennial
Url: https://thepostmillennial.com/biden-authorized-235-million-
in-funding-to-palestinians-one-month-before-hamas-attacks-
on-israel
Date retrieved: June 3 2020

10   Title: "Google Diversity Chief Kamau Bobb: 'Jews Have Insatiable
Appetite for War and Killing'"
Author: Allum Bokhari
Date: June 2, 2021
Title of Publication: Breitbart
Url: https://www.breitbart.com/tech/2021/06/02/google-diver-
sity-chief-kamau-bobb-jews-have-insatiable-appetite-for-war-
and-killing/
Date retrieved: June 4, 2021

11   Title: "Liberals cant be silent as the left incites anti-Semitism"
Author: Jonathan S. Tobin
Date: May 23, 2021
Title of Publication: The Algemeiner

Url: https://www.algemeiner.com/2021/05/23/
liberals-cant-be-silent-as-the-left-incites-antisemitism/
Date retrieved: June 5, 2021

12   Title: "What Ilhan Omar Said About 9/11 Will Have You
Fuming Mad"
Author: Dnaiel
Date: April 10, 2019
Title of Publication: Freedom Headlines
Url: https://freedomheadlines.com/freedom-wire/
what-ilhan-omar-said-about-9-11-will-have-you-fuming-mad/
Date retrieved: June 5, 2021

13   Title: "Crowder: Here's proof Rashida Tlaib supports terrorism"
Author: Steven Crowder
Date: August 22, 2019
Title of Publication: Blaze Media
Url: https://www.theblaze.com/steven-crowder/tlaib-terrorism
Date retrieved: June 5, 2021

14   Title: "House Republicans Troll AOC After She Calls Israel an
'Apartheid State'"
Author: Reagan McCarthy
Date: May 21, 2021
Title of Publication: Town Hall
Url: https://townhall.com/tipsheet/reaganmccarthy/2021/05/21/
waltz-trolls-aoc-on-israel-n2589832
Date retrieved: June 5, 2021

15   Title: "PALESTINIANS REJECTED STATEHOOD THREE TIMES,
CLAIM FRUSTRATION — WITH ISRAEL"
Author: Alex Safian
Date: September 22, 2022
Title of Publication: Camera
Url: https://www.camera.org/article/palestinians-rejected-state-
hood-three-times-claim-frustration-with-israel/
Date retrieved: June 5, 2021

16 Title: "Mayor Ted Wheeler"
Author: Unknown
Date: Unknown
Title of Publication: Portland.gov
Url: https://www.portland.gov/wheeler
Date retrieved: June 5, 2021

17 Title: "Carlson Tweets List Of 100 Things The Left Claimed Were "Racist" In 2017"
Author: Mike LaChance
Date: December 24, 2017
Title of Publication: American Lookout
Url: https://americanlookout.com/tucker-carlson-tweets-list-of-100-things-the-left-claimed-were-racist-in-2017/
Date retrieved: June 6, 2021

18 Title: "CDC shows COVID-19 has high survival rate; doctor still wants to see precautions taken"
Author: Taylor Smith
Date: September 26, 2020
Title of Publication: Wink News
Url: https://www.winknews.com/2020/09/23/cdc-shows-covid-19-has-high-survival-rate-doctor-still-wants-to-see-precautions-taken/
Date retrieved: June 6, 2021

19 Title: "Vaccine reduces severity, not shield against Covid-19, say experts"
Author: Unknown
Date: April 16, 2021
Title of Publication: Deccan Herald
Url: https://www.deccanherald.com/national/north-and-central/vaccine-reduces-severity-not-shield-against-covid-19-say-experts-974894.html
Date retrieved: June 6, 2021

20 Title: "Good news: Mild COVID-19 induces lasting antibody
    protection"
    Author: Tamara Bhandari
    Date: May 24, 2021
    Title of Publication: Washington University in St. Louis,
    The Source
    Url: https://source.wustl.edu/2021/05/
    good-news-mild-covid-19-induces-lasting-antibody-protection/
    Date retrieved: June 6, 2021

21 Title: "Latest Data on COVID-19 Vaccinations by Race/Ethnicity"
    Author: Nambi Ndugga, LaToya Hill, Samantha Artiga, and
    Noah Parker
    Date: June 7, 2021
    Title of Publication: KFF
    Url: https://www.kff.org/coronavirus-covid-19/issue-brief/
    latest-data-on-covid-19-vaccinations-race-ethnicity/
    Date retrieved: June 7, 2021

22 Title: "Tuskegee Syphilis Study"
    Author: The Editors of Encyclopedia Britannica
    Date: Unknown
    Title of Publication: Britainnica.com
    Url: https://www.britannica.com/event/Tuskegee-syphilis-study
    Date retrieved: June 7, 2021

23 Title: "Austin Pledges New National Defense Strategy; Commits
    To Strong Civilian Leadership"
    Author: Paul McLeary
    Date: January 19, 2021
    Title of Publication: Breaking Defense
    Url: https://breakingdefense.com/2021/01/austin-pledg-
    es-new-national-defense-strategy-commits-to-strong-civil-
    ian-leadership/
    Date retrieved: June 8, 2021

24   Title: "COVID-19 situation report: The latest coronavirus updates from the US military"
Author: Paul Szoldra
Date: March 27, 2020
Title of Publication: Task and Purpose
Url: https://taskandpurpose.com/news/covid-19-military/
Date retrieved: June 8, 2021

25   Title: "Military suicide deaths rose 25% at the end of 2020: Report"
Author: Mica Soellner
Date: April 6, 2021
Title of Publication: Washington Examiner
Url: https://www.washingtonexaminer.com/news/military-suicides-up-in-last-months-of-2020
Date retrieved: June 8, 2021

26   Title: "Military Deaths by Suicide Jumped 25% at End of 2020"
Author: Stephen Losey
Date: April 5, 2021
Title of Publication: April 21, 2021
Url: https://www.military.com/daily-news/2021/04/05/military-deaths-suicide-jumped-25-end-of-2020.html
Date retrieved: June 8, 2021

27   Title: "Rand Paul Confronts Dr. Fauci for His hand in 'Gain in Function' Research"
Author: Unknown
Date: May 11, 2021
Title of Publication: Worthy Watch
Url: https://worthy.watch/ran-paul-confronts-dr-fauci
Date retrieved: June 8, 2021

28   Title: "Why Does Fauci Hold Patents on a Key HIV Component Used to Create COVID-19"
Author: The Beat Man
Date: July 9, 2020
Title of Publication: Living in Anglo America

Url: https://angloamerica101.wordpress.com/2020/07/09/why-does-fauci-hold-patents-on-a-key-hiv-component-used-to-create-covid-19/
Date retrieved: June 9, 2021

29   Title: "Joe Rogan won't take COVID-19 vaccine: 'I would if I felt like I needed it'"
Author: Karim Zidan
Date: February 1, 2021
Title of Publication: Bloody Elbow
Url: https://www.bloodyelbow.com/2021/2/1/22260630/joe-rogan-coronavirus-vaccine-disinformation-spotify-jre-mma-news
Date retrieved: June 9, 2021

30   Title: "Wrong Again: 50 Years of Failed Eco-pocalyptic Predictions
Author: Myron Ebell
Date: September 18, 2019
Title of Publication: Competitive Enterprise Institute
Url: https://cei.org/blog/wrong-again-50-years-of-failed-eco-pocalyptic-predictions/
Date retrieved: June 9, 2021

31   Title: "The Tragedy Of Greta Thunberg"
Author: David Harsanyi
Date: September 23, 2019
Title of Publication: The Federalist
Url: https://thefederalist.com/2019/09/23/the-tragedy-of-greta-thunberg/
Date retrieved: June 9, 2021

32   Title: "'Fear Sells': CNN Lauds 'Climate Crisis' Town Hall After Panic Porn Agenda Exposed"
Author: Joseph Vazquez
Date: April 22, 2021
Title of Publication: mrc NewsBusters

Url: https://www.newsbusters.org/blogs/
business/joseph-vazquez/2021/04/22/
fear-sells-cnn-lauds-climate-crisis-town-hall-after-panic
Date retrieved: June 10, 2021

33   Title: "Climate Science's Myth Buster"
Author: Guy Sorman
Date: Winter, 2019
Title of Publication: Cityjournal.org
Url: https://www.city-journal.org/global-warming
Date retrieved: June 9, 2021

34   Title: "4 Reasons Trump Was Right to Pull Out of the Paris
Agreement"
Author: Nicolas Loris and Katie Tubb
Date: June 1, 2017
Title of Publication: The Heritage Foundation
Url: https://www.heritage.org/environment/commentary/4-rea-
sons-trump-was-right-pull-out-the-paris-agreement
Date retrieved: June 9, 2021

35   Title: "Greenhouse effect is a myth, say scientists"
Author: Julie Wheldon
Date: March, 2007
Title of Publication: Dailymail.com
Url: https://www.dailymail.co.uk/sciencetech/article-440049/
Greenhouse-effect-myth-say-scientists.html
Date retrieved: June 9, 2021

36   Title: "How eating insects could help climate change"
Author: Unknown
Date: December 11, 2015
Title of Publication: BBCNews.com
Url: https://www.bbc.com/news/av/
science-environment-35061609
Date retrieved: June 10, 2021

37   Title: "Johns Hopkins Psychiatrist: Transgender is 'Mental Disorder;' Sex Change 'Biologically Impossible'"
     Author: Michael W. Chapman
     Date: November 26, 2020
     Title of Publication: CNS News
     Url: https://www.cnsnews.com/article/national/michael-w-chapman/johns-hopkins-psychiatrist-transgender-mental-disorder-sex
     Date retrieved: June 10, 2021

38   Title: "What Percentage of Transgenders Regret Surgery?"
     Author: Susan Ciancio
     Date: July 7, 2021
     Title of Publication: Human Life International
     Url: https://www.hli.org/resources/what-percentage-of-transgenders-regret-surgery/
     Date retrieved: June 10, 2021

39   Title: "Your Fat Stigma Is Racist – Here Are 6 Ways to Shift That"
     Author: Caleb Luna
     Date: January 22, 2017
     Title of Publication: EverydayFeminism.com
     Url: https://everydayfeminism.com/2017/01/how-to-shift-racist-fat-stigma/
     Date retrieved: June 10, 2021

40   Title: "CDC study finds about 78% of people hospitalized for Covid were overweight or obese"
     Author: Berkeley Lovelace, Jr.
     Date: March 9, 2021
     Title of Publication: CNBC.com
     Url: https://www.cnbc.com/2021/03/08/covid-cdc-study-finds-roughly-78percent-of-people-hospitalized-were-overweight-or-obese.html
     Date retrieved: June 10, 2021

41   Title: "Life Begins at Fertilization: 96% of Liberal, Pro-Choice and Non-Religious Biologists Agree"
Author: Zachary Mettler
Date: October 22, 2019
Title of Publication: The Daily Citizen
Url: https://dailycitizen.focusonthefamily.com/life-begins-at-fertilization-96-of-liberal-pro-choice-and-non-religious-biologists-agree/
Date retrieved: June 10, 2021

42   Title: "Yes, Democrats DID start the Ku Klux Klan (and it's still the party of racism)"
Author: Joe Jarvis
Date: February 7, 2019
Title of Publication: The Daily Bell
Url: https://www.thedailybell.com/all-articles/news-analysis/yes-democrats-did-start-the-ku-klux-klan-and-its-still-the-party-of-racism/
Date retrieved: June 10, 2021

43   Title: "Obama's Father's Day remarks"
Author: Unknown
Date: June 15, 2008
Title of Publication: The New York Times
Url: https://www.nytimes.com/2008/06/15/us/politics/15text-obama.html
Date retrieved: June 10, 2021

44   Title: "Exclusive: Black Leader Recruits for Grassroots Critical Race Theory Pushback"
Author: Dr. Susan Berry
Date: June 2, 2021
Title of Publication: Breitbart
Url: https://www.breitbart.com/politics/2021/06/02/exclusive-black-leader-recruits-for-grassroots-critical-race-theory-pushback/
Date retrieved: June 10, 2021

45   Title: "The Worst Enemy of Black People According to Malcolm X"
Author: Walter Williams
Date: February 6, 2020
Title of Publication: Capitalism Magazine
Url: https://www.capitalismmagazine.com/2020/02/
the-worst-enemy-of-black-people-according-to-malcolm-x/
Date retrieved: June 10, 2021

46   Title: "The Truth About the 12.5 Million Black Slaves Kidnapped
out of Africa"
Author: Larry Elder
Date: June 2, 2021
Title of Publication: The Epoch Times
Url: https://www.theepochtimes.com/the-truth-about-the-
12-5-million-black-slaves-kidnapped-out-of-africa-larry-
elder_3840687.html
Date retrieved: June 10, 2021

47   Title: "Where Did Millions of Dollars in Donations to Black Lives
Matter Go?"
Author: Katie Pavlich
Date: February 24, 2021
Title of Publication: Townhall
Url: https://townhall.com/tipsheet/katiepavlich/2021/02/24/
where-did-millions-of-dollars-in-donations-to-black-lives-mat-
ter-go-n2585249
Date retrieved: June 10, 2021

48   Title: "George Soros's Foundation Pours $220 Million Into Racial
Equality Push"
Author: Astead Herndon
Date: June 13, 2020
Title of Publication: The New York Times
Url: https://www.nytimes.com/2020/07/13/us/politics/george-so-
ros-racial-justice-organizations.html
Date retrieved: June 11, 2021

49 Title: "Biden: 'Terrorism from White Supremacy Is the Most Lethal Threat to the Homeland Today, Not ISIS, Not Al Qaeda'"
Author: Susan Jones
Date: June 2, 2021
Title of Publication: CNSnews.com
Url: https://www.cnsnews.com/index.php/article/national/susan-jones/biden-terrorism-white-supremacy-most-lethal-threat-homeland-today-not
Date retrieved: June 11, 2021

50 Title: "DOJ Report: For Black Victims of Violent Crime, 70.3% of Offenders Are Fellow Blacks, 10.6% of Offenders Are White"
Author: Michael W. Chapman
Date: April 15, 2021
Title of Publication: CNSnews.com
Url: https://cnsnews.com/article/national/michael-w-chapman/doj-report-black-victims-violent-crime-703-offenders-are-fellow
Date retrieved: June 11, 2021

51 Title: "Letter from Margaret Sanger to Dr. C.J. Gamble"
Author: Margaret Sanger
Date: December 10, 1939
Title of Publication: Genius.com
Url: https://genius.com/Margaret-sanger-letter-from-margaret-sanger-to-dr-cj-gamble-annotated
Date retrieved: June 11, 2021

52 Title: "Watch Hillary Praise Planned Parenthood's Eugenicist Founder Margaret Sanger"
Author: Sean Davis
Date: June 14, 2015
Title of Publication: The Federalist
Url: https://thefederalist.com/2015/07/14/watch-hillary-praise-planned-parenthoods-eugenicist-founder-margaret-sanger/
Date retrieved: June 11, 2021

53   Title: "Prefrontal Cortex: Definition, Role, Development & More"
Author: Hannah Grace
Date: 2020
Title of Publication: TypesofTherapy.com
Url: https://www.typesoftherapy.com/
prefrontal-cortex-definition-role-development/
Date retrieved: June 11, 2021

54   Title: "Winston S. Churchill > Quotes > Quotable Quote"
Author: Winston S. Churchill
Date: Unknown
Title of Publication: Goodreads.com
Url: https://www.goodreads.com/
quotes/7441607-any-man-under-30-who-is-not-a-liberal-has
Date retrieved: June 11, 2021

55   Title: "How the Progressive Left Ruined Education"
Author: Wen Wyrte
Date: September 6, 2020
Title of Publication: American Thinker
Url: https://www.americanthinker.com/articles/2020/09/how_the_
progressive_left_ruined_education.html
Date retrieved: June 11, 2021

56   Title: "Education Department Proposal Would Flood Public
Schools With Woke Curricula"
Author: Alex Nester
Date: April 21, 2021
Title of Publication: The Washington Free Beacon
Url: https://freebeacon.com/biden-administration/education-de-
partment-proposal-would-flood-public-schools-with-woke-curri
cula/c
Date retrieved: June 11, 2021

57   Title: "Oregon Pushes Idea That Math Is Racist, Encourages
Teachers to Dismantle White Supremacy"
Author: Kipp Jones
Date: February 12, 2021

Title of Publication: The Western Journal
Url: https://www.westernjournal.com/oregon-push-es-idea-math-racist-encourages-teachers-disman-tle-white-supremacy/
Date retrieved: June 11, 2021

58 Title: "California promotes 'dismantling racism in mathematics' guidance in draft for statewide framework"
Author: Sam Dorman
Date: April 14, 2021
Title of Publication: FoxNews.com
Url: https://www.foxnews.com/us/california-racism-math-framework
Date retrieved: June 12, 2021

59 Title: "Dad says NYC DOE public schools are 'brainwashing' kids with woke agenda"
Author: Anonymous
Date: January 30, 2021
Title of Publication: New York Post
Url: https://nypost.com/2021/01/30/dad-says-nyc-doe-public-schools-are-brainwashing-kids/
Date retrieved: June 12, 2021

60 Title: "The Myth of the Gender Wage Gap"
Author: Christina Hoff Sommers
Date: September 22, 2014
Title of Publication: Prager U
Url: https://www.prageru.com/video/the-myth-of-the-gender-wage-gap/
Date retrieved: June 12, 2021

61 Title: "Researchers: PTSD Rates Increased by 61 Percent After Abortion"
Author: Unknown
Date: February 13, 2008
Title of Publication: Lifesitenews.com

Url: https://www.lifesitenews.com/news/
researchers-ptsd-rates-increased-by-61-percent-after-abortion/
Date retrieved: June 12, 2021

62 Title: "18 Shocking Abortion Statistics Rape Victims"
Author: Unknown
Date: Unknown
Title of Publication: Healthresearchfunding.org
Url: https://healthresearchfunding.
org/18-shocking-abortion-statistics-rape-victims/
Date retrieved: June 12, 2021

63 Title: "Mothers Have an Impact That Goes Far Beyond Their
Families"
Author: Kay C. James
Date: May 6, 2020
Title of Publication: The Heritage Foundation
Url: https://www.heritage.org/marriage-and-family/commentary/
mothers-have-impact-goes-far-beyond-their-families
Date retrieved: June 12, 2021

64 Title: "Transgender MMA Fighter Who Fractured a Woman's Skull,
Named 'Bravest Athlete in History'"
Author: Penny Starr
Date: January 22, 2020
Title of Publication: Breitbart
Url: https://www.breitbart.com/sports/2020/01/22/transgender-
mma-fighter-who-fractured-womans-skull-named-bravest-ath-
lete-history/
Date retrieved: June 12, 2021

65 Title: "Hunter Biden's Racist Text Messages Revealed Just Days
After Joe Biden Lectured Americans on Racism: Report"
Author: Kipp Jones
Date: June 8, 2021
Title of Publication: The Western Journal

Url: https://www.westernjournal.com/hunter-bidens-racist-text-messages-revealed-just-days-joe-biden-lectured-americans-racism-report/
Date retrieved: June 12, 2021

66 Title: "Billie Eilish Addresses Racism Accusations: 'I'm Being Labeled Something That I Am Not'"
Author: Naledi Ushe
Date: June 8, 2021
Title of Publication: Yahoo.com
Url: https://www.yahoo.com/now/billie-eilish-addresses-racism-accusations-041257102.html
Date retrieved: June 12, 2021

67 Title: "Virtue-signaling soccer star Megan Rapinoe — who tells others 'we have to be better' — stereotypes Asians in resurfaced tweet"
Author: Dave Urbanski
Date: June 17, 2021
Title of Publication: Blaze Media
Url: https://www.theblaze.com/news/virtue-signaling-megan-rapinoe-stereotypes-asians
Date retrieved: June 18, 2021

68 Title: "Washington Gov. Inslee Signs Bill Requiring Critical Race Training For Public School Teachers"
Author: Jeff Reynolds
Date: May 9, 2021
Title of Publication: Legal Insurrection
Url: https://legalinsurrection.com/2021/05/washington-gov-inslee-signs-bill-requiring-critical-race-training-for-public-school-teachers/
Date retrieved: June 19, 2021

69 Title: "Biden has embraced lunatic 'critical race theory' — but you can still fight it"
Author: Max Eden
Date: January 25, 2021

Title of Publication: The New York Post
Url: https://nypost.com/2021/01/25/biden-has-embraced-luna-tic-critical-race-theory-but-you-can-still-fight-it/
Date retrieved: June 19, 2021

70   Title: "Study: 46 Out of 47 European Countries Require Photo ID to Vote"
Author: Guy Benson
Date: June 4, 2021
Title of Publication: Town Hall
Url: https://townhall.com/tipsheet/guybenson/2021/06/04/study-46-out-of-47-european-countries-require-photo-id-to-vote-n2590454
Date retrieved: June 19, 2021

71   Title: "24 things that require a photo ID"
Author: Ashe Schow
Date: August 14, 2013
Title of Publication: Washington Examiner
Url: https://www.washingtonexaminer.com/24-things-that-require-a-photo-id
Date retrieved: June 19, 2021

72   No title
Author: No author
Date: No date
Title of Publication: Quotefancy.com
Url: https://quotefancy.com/quote/920802/Thomas-Sowell-Racism-is-not-dead-but-it-is-on-life-support-kept-alive-by-politicians-race
Date retrieved: June 19, 2021

73   Title: "NEGATIVE EFFECTS OF SOY ON MEN"
Author: Unknown
Date: September 12, 2019
Title of Publication: The Mas Clinic
Url: https://themasclinic.com/negative-effects-of-soy-on-men/
Date retrieved: June 19, 2021

74   Title: "Army disables crush of critical comments on 'woke' recruitment videos"
Author: Ben Wolfgang
Date: May 21, 2021
Title of Publication: The Washington Times
Url: https://www.washingtontimes.com/news/2021/may/21/army-disables-crush-critical-comments-woke-recruit/
Date retrieved: June 20, 2021

75   Title: "Russian Military Recruitment Video"
Author: Unknown
Date: Unknown
Url: https://vimeo.com/334102304
Date retrieved: June 20, 2021

76   Title: "GOP's Cotton and Crenshaw seek military whistleblowers on 'woke ideology'"
Author: May Kay Linge
Date: May 29, 2021
Title of Publication: New York Post
Url: https://nypost.com/2021/05/29/gops-cotton-crenshaw-seek-military-whistleblowers-on-woke-ideology/
Date retrieved: June 20, 2021

77   Title: "Quotations of the Day from Thomas Sowell"
Author: Mark J. Perry
Date: June 26, 2020
Title of Publication: AEI
Url: https://www.aei.org/carpe-diem/quotations-of-the-day-from-thomas-sowell-3/
Date retrieved: June 20, 2021

78   Title: "WHAT DOES IT MEAN TO BE A REAL MAN?"
Author: Unknown
Date: August 26, 2015
Title of Publication: Patching Cracks
Url: https://patchingcracks.com/2015/08/26/what-does-it-mean-to-be-a-real-man/

Date retrieved: June 20, 2021

79   Title: "The Declaration of Independence"
Title of Publication: National Archives
Url: https://www.archives.gov/founding-docs/declaration
Date retrieved: June 20, 2021